World War II Quest

A Time-Travel Adventure Through World History

Jane Vera

© **Copyright 2024 - All rights reserved.**

The content contained within this book may not be reproduced, duplicated or transmitted without direct written permission from the author or the publisher.

Under no circumstances will any blame or legal responsibility be held against the publisher, or author, for any damages, reparation, or monetary loss due to the information contained within this book, either directly or indirectly.

Legal Notice:

This book is copyright protected. It is only for personal use. You cannot amend, distribute, sell, use, quote or paraphrase any part, or the content within this book, without the consent of the author or publisher.

Disclaimer Notice:

Please note the information contained within this document is for educational and entertainment purposes only. All effort has been executed to present accurate, up to date, reliable, complete information. No warranties of any kind are declared or implied. Readers acknowledge that the author is not engaged in the rendering of legal, financial, medical or professional advice. The content within this book has been derived from various sources. Please consult a licensed professional before attempting any techniques outlined in this book.

By reading this document, the reader agrees that under no circumstances is the author responsible for any losses, direct or indirect, that are incurred as a result of the use of the information contained within this document, including, but not limited to, errors, omissions, or inaccuracies.

Table of Contents

INTRODUCTION 1

CHAPTER 1: THE MYSTERIOUS MUSEUM 3
    No More Screen Time on a Holiday Too?! 3
    At the Museum 5
    The Magic Clock in the Secret Chamber 6
    Do You Know? 8
    Key Words 9
    Quiz 10

CHAPTER 2: THE TIME TRAVEL TWIST 13
    What Could the Note Mean? 13
    Only One Way to Find Out 14
    Do You Know? 16
    Key Words 17
    Quiz 19

CHAPTER 3: THE BLITZ EXPERIENCE 23
    London, 1940 23
    How Did It All Start? What Can We Do? 25
    What Next? 26
    Do You Know? 27
    Key Words 28
    Quiz 30

CHAPTER 4: THE BATTLE OF BRITAIN AND WINSTON CHURCHILL 33
    The British Bulldog 33
    The Battle of Britain—Aerial Warfare 35
    Do You Know? 36
    Key Words 37
    Quiz 39

CHAPTER 5: SPIES AND CODEBREAKERS AT BLETCHLEY PARK 43
    Bletchley Park 43
    Station X 45
    Just in the Nick of Time 46
    Do You Know? 47

KEY WORDS	48
QUIZ	51

CHAPTER 6: WOMEN AT WAR 55

THE MUNITIONS FACTORY	55
WOMEN IN THE WAR	56
DO YOU KNOW?	57
KEY WORDS	59
QUIZ	61

CHAPTER 7: PEARL HARBOR AND AMERICA ENTERS THE WAR 65

A SNEAK ATTACK	65
DAY OF INFAMY	67
DO YOU KNOW?	68
KEY WORDS	69
QUIZ	70

CHAPTER 8: THE BATTLE OF MIDWAY 73

OPERATION MI	73
THE BATTLE OF MIDWAY—NAVAL WARFARE	74
DO YOU KNOW?	75
KEY WORDS	76
QUIZ	77

CHAPTER 9: THE BATTLE OF EL ALAMEIN 81

THE SECOND BATTLE OF EL ALAMEIN—DESERT AND GROUND WARFARE	82
Operation Lightfoot	*82*
Operation Supercharge	*83*
DO YOU KNOW?	84
KEY WORDS	86
QUIZ	88

CHAPTER 10: D-DAY AND THE LIBERATION OF FRANCE 91

THE BATTLE OF NORMANDY	91
VIVA LA PARIS	93
DO YOU KNOW?	94
KEY WORDS	95
QUIZ	96

CHAPTER 11: THE HOLOCAUST 99

BUCHENWALD, APRIL 11, 1945	99
THE HORRORS OF THE HOLOCAUST	101
DO YOU KNOW?	102
KEY WORDS	104

    QUIZ 106

CHAPTER 12: IN BERLIN AT THE END OF THE WAR 109

    BERLIN'S SURRENDER AND THE TWO V-DAYS 109
    THE LAST DAYS OF THE DICTATOR 111
    BERLIN'S FALL AND GERMANY'S PARTITION 112
    DO YOU KNOW? 112
    KEY WORDS 113
    QUIZ 114

CHAPTER 13: THE MANHATTAN PROJECT 117

    THE SECRET PROJECT—MANHATTAN PROJECT 117
    LOS ALAMOS—PROJECT Y 118
    THE PEOPLE 119
    DO YOU KNOW? 120
    KEY WORDS 121
    QUIZ 122

CHAPTER 14: THE COLD WAR BEGINS 125

    THE COLD WAR (1950–1990) 125
    NATO 126
    DO YOU KNOW? 127
    KEY WORDS 128
    QUIZ 129

CHAPTER 15: BACK TO THE PRESENT 133

    TIME'S RUNNING OUT 133
    BACK TO THE HERE AND NOW 134
    A NEW APPRECIATION 135

HISTORICAL NOTES 137

    A TIMELINE OF EVENTS 137
        1933–1939: Prelude to World War II 137
        1939–1945: World War II 138
        Post-War Era (1945–1950) 141
        The Cold War (1950–1990) 142
        1991: The End of the Cold War 143

CONCLUSION 145

ABOUT THE AUTHOR 147

QUIZ ANSWERS **153**

Chapter 1 153
Chapter 2 153
Chapter 3 154
Chapter 4 154
Chapter 5 155
Chapter 6 155
Chapter 7 156
Chapter 8 156
Chapter 9 157
Chapter 10 157
Chapter 11 158
Chapter 12 158
Chapter 13 159
Chapter 14 159

REFERENCES **161**

Introduction

Eleven-year-old Tim and his younger sister, Maya were excited. They live in New York and a long weekend was coming up, with Monday being a holiday for Memorial Day. Tim already had plans for the time off from school. He would play games online all day in his room, do a bit of watercolor in the new book his dad got him, and catch up on homework (to keep his mom off his back).

Maya, too, had plans. She had narrowed down a series on Netflix she wanted to binge-watch and finish. Her friends were all already halfway through it, and discussions of it always seemed to leave her out simply because she hadn't watched it yet.

What Tim and Maya don't know yet is that there are bigger things in store for them over the weekend. You see, things are just not going to work out as per their plans! In a strange time travel twist, they will be a part of World War II and see the events that shaped it first-hand. They are going to get so involved in their adventure that they won't even think about their video game and TV series once!

But they need your help, dear reader! Yes, that's right! You will be the one partnering with them and helping them on their journey, from one country to another. They and you will learn how the Second World War affected the common people, the reasons why it started, how the world was broken into two factions over it, how it ended, and how the world still went on fighting for a long time even after the war! You will also understand an important lesson—the absence of war need not always mean peace.

With Tim and Maya, you will meet not just the great leaders who changed the path of human history but also ordinary people who bravely stood up for what they thought was right. You will meet Holocaust survivors, women without whom the war could not have been won, and soldiers who laid down their lives for their countries. You will see battles waged in the air, sea, and on land!

As you would tell me, history is not always interesting to read, with its long list of people, dates, and places to remember. But what if you were right in the middle of what was happening? What if you could see everything up close? Would you still find it all so forgettable?

History is important because it has shaped our times, our lives, and even the technology and things we use more than we can see. WWII, in particular, changed our lives because it was the biggest war fought. Suddenly, we realized that the world could be destroyed with the push of a button and that nothing could be worth that!

This book will certainly change your outlook on history and wars. Even in the most serious of times, human beings have found courage, faith, and even fun! So can you!

Treat this book like a story and you will be rewarded with a wealth of information on the war that made even the Great War (WW I) before that small by comparison. In the coming pages, you will learn

- the story of the Second World War from the eyes of two children like you.
- interesting snippets of information, trivia, and facts on people, events, and places that changed the course of history.

There are even quizzes for you to test your knowledge and find out more about the period and events. Answers to these are, of course, provided at the end of the book. However, you mustn't be in a hurry to flip to them without giving the questions an honest try first!

All the best, reader-traveler! *Bon voyage* and a safe return to you! You are about to plunge into an information-packed, adventure-loaded quest!

Chapter 1:

The Mysterious Museum

No More Screen Time on a Holiday Too?!

Tim yawned, and a casual glance at the clock on the mantelpiece told him it was almost 8.00 a.m. For a moment, he panicked—was he about to be late for school again? And then the blissful awareness dawned on him: It was a holiday weekend! In fact, it was only Saturday, the first of three days for which he would be rid of all schoolwork. Monday was Memorial Day—some memorial thing for soldiers or something. Whatever it was, it was a great time to finish the next level of *Roblox* he was playing against his friends. He really wanted to come in first this time.

In the next room, Maya was already up. She was humming a Taylor Swift song under her breath, thinking about the Netflix action animated series *Carmen Sandiego* that all her friends had already watched.

3

Maya's mom had been a little hesitant to let her watch it because someone had told her it was "too violent for kids." Now that Maya was 10, her mom told her she could watch it as long as her schoolwork was on track, of course. And Maya was determined to finish it over the weekend. She could complete schoolwork around watching it—of that, she was sure.

But Mom had a shocker for them over the breakfast table.

As she was piling pancakes onto their plates, she said, "Well, today I have a little something for you guys. A break from the monotony of screens."

Tim and Maya did not often agree on everything, but today there was a combined groan, "Noooooo! Mom, but it is a holiday!"

Mom said firmly, "No buts. We are going to the museum today, where they have a special exhibition on World War II. I want us all to be there."

Maya said, "War is made by and for men! It's so boring to look at all those machines, guns, and whatnot!"

Tim said, "World War II? You gotta be kidding! That was like some million years ago! Why should we be interested?"

Mom said, "It was only 85 years ago, Tim. Your Nana is 95! And Maya, you'll see when we get there."

The children sulked but had no choice.

In the car, on the way, Tim whispered to Maya, "Let's just pretend to be bored throughout, okay? Hopefully, Mom will bring us home earlier if she realizes we have no interest in any of it."

Maya held his outstretched palm in solidarity and nodded gravely. It was a secret sibling pact.

At the Museum

Despite their agreement, Tim and Maya did not realize time slipping away at the museum. Tim was fascinated by the weapons and vehicles the armies used. Maya gasped at the photos of women who served in combat and worked as nurses and in factories during the war.

Mom smiled as Tim asked their guide at the museum, "But did you not say the war in Africa? How many places was this war fought?"

The guide, a spectacled man named John, said, "That's right. The Second World War was fought all over the world. The European, Pacific, North African, and Eastern Theaters were all part of the war. Battles were fought in many European countries, the Pacific islands and parts of Asia, North African colonies, the Soviet Union, the Balkans, and the Baltic States."

Maya asked him, "And you say this happened across six years?"

John said, "Yes. The war raged from 1939 to 1945 between the Allied Powers of the UK, USA, France, and the Soviets or Russia on one side and the Axis Forces of Germany, Italy, and Japan, on the other. It started when Germany, under the Nazis, invaded Poland, and Britain and France declared war on Germany in response. Our country joined the war later, in December 1941, after Pearl Harbor was attacked."

The children were amazed and asked many more questions. They couldn't imagine the whole world being torn apart in two like that. It seemed impossible to even think the US could be under threat of an invasion!

Finally, John smiled, bid them adieu, and told them he had to leave, but they could look around.

When Mom said, "Let's go," Tim and Maya still weren't finished looking at the mini models of the tanks, anti-aircraft guns, and armored vans. They wanted to see the uniforms of the soldiers and more photos of the soldiers and cities from the period.

Mom finally said, pointing at the clock in the foyer, "Alright, you two, see that clock there? If we don't leave by 12, we'll run late for lunch at Bleecker Street."

Tim and Maya were distracted for a minute by the mention of their favorite pizza place in New York City but quickly nodded at her and continued looking at the things on display.

As Tim reached one particular section about "America in the war," he excitedly drew out his hand from his pocket so fast that he accidentally pulled out the crazy ball he always carried about. The ball bounced off the floor and rolled off behind a shelf. He squeezed between the shelf and the wall to retrieve it and saw something that thrilled him.

He called out, "Hey! Look at this, Maya!"

The Magic Clock in the Secret Chamber

When Maya came beside him, he was pushing with all his might against what looked like a secret door in the wall behind the shelf. Maya was, by nature, more cautious.

She said, "I don't think you should be doing that, Tim. I mean, we could ask one of the staff..."

Tim cut her short, saying, "No way! This is a secret door! It looks just like the wall. If I hadn't pushed into this lever here by mistake, I wouldn't have seen it. You can come with me, or I'll just go on my own."

"Okay, okay. I'll come." Maya shrugged, looked around, and slowly slid into the gap between the wall and the shelf. She certainly did not want Tim to go and get into trouble. A part of her did not want to miss the adventure either.

The two slowly pushed past the door into an old dusty chamber. As they walked into the dark room, Tim discovered an old grandfather clock at the end of the tiny room. That was the only other thing, apart from them, that was there. They looked at each other and found disappointment mirrored in each other's faces. After all this effort, it seemed they were in just an old storage cabinet!

Maya walked to the clock and dusted it with her hand to find that it had a gold-colored frame. She knew it would look quite stunning if cleaned properly.

"It's pretty," she said. "Wonder why they left it in this moldy, dusty place."

Tim cried, "Wait a sec..." He was excitedly pulling at and rattling the trunk of the clock.

"Tim," hissed Maya, "What do you think you're doing? You'll break it, and we'll probably be grounded forever."

Tim continued at it until the door of the grandfather clock swung open. On the floor of the clock, below the weights and pendulum, lay a piece of parchment paper. There were words written on it in an ancient hand.

Maya bent down, picked it up, and read it in the dim light. The note said

With each turn of the dial, a decade unfolds,

The Clock holds time's mysterious stories.

Wind it back, whispering the time and place you want to be,

To journey through history's ancient trail.

Tim and Maya read through it again, and their faces lit up. Did the note really mean what they think it did?

Do You Know?

World War II lasted for exactly six years, starting on September 1, 1939, and ending on September 2, 1945. It wasn't always called "World War II." The First World War (1914–1918) was initially called the "Great War" or the "European War" until America entered in 1917. It then became called the "World War." Since nobody could predict that another such war would come, "World War II" was not used at the time, much like how we might refer to the possibility of a "Third World War" today. American President Franklin D. Roosevelt called it the Second World War publicly in 1941 and the name stuck.

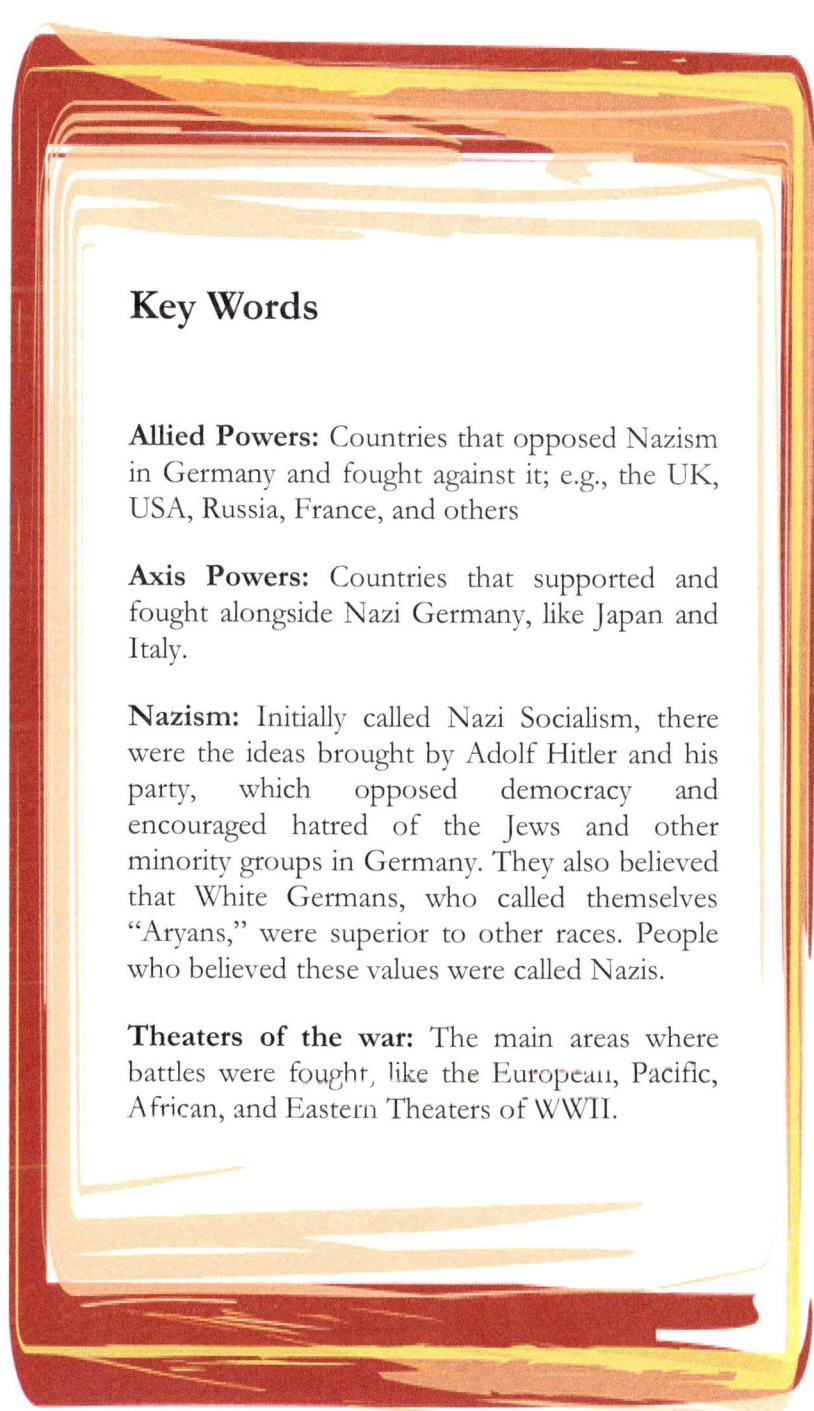

Key Words

Allied Powers: Countries that opposed Nazism in Germany and fought against it; e.g., the UK, USA, Russia, France, and others

Axis Powers: Countries that supported and fought alongside Nazi Germany, like Japan and Italy.

Nazism: Initially called Nazi Socialism, there were the ideas brought by Adolf Hitler and his party, which opposed democracy and encouraged hatred of the Jews and other minority groups in Germany. They also believed that White Germans, who called themselves "Aryans," were superior to other races. People who believed these values were called Nazis.

Theaters of the war: The main areas where battles were fought, like the European, Pacific, African, and Eastern Theaters of WWII.

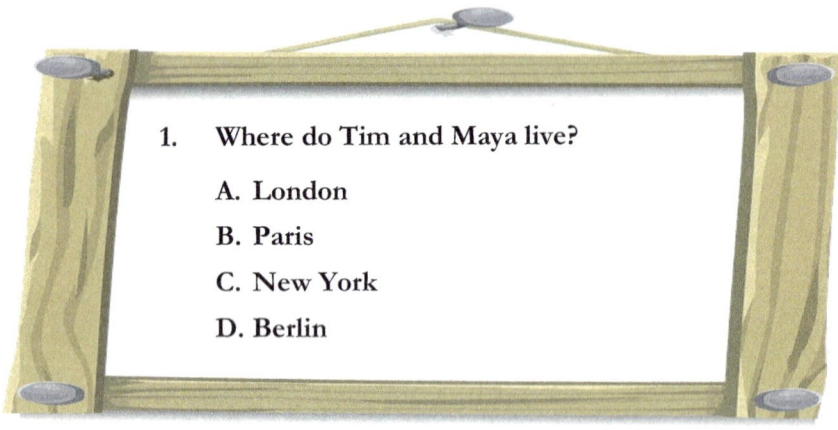

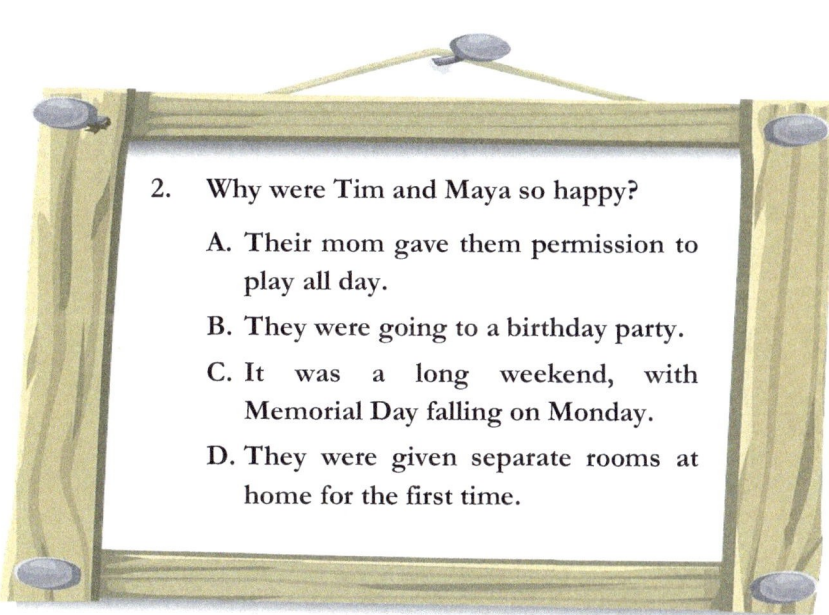

2. Why were Tim and Maya so happy?

   A. Their mom gave them permission to play all day.
   B. They were going to a birthday party.
   C. It was a long weekend, with Memorial Day falling on Monday.
   D. They were given separate rooms at home for the first time.

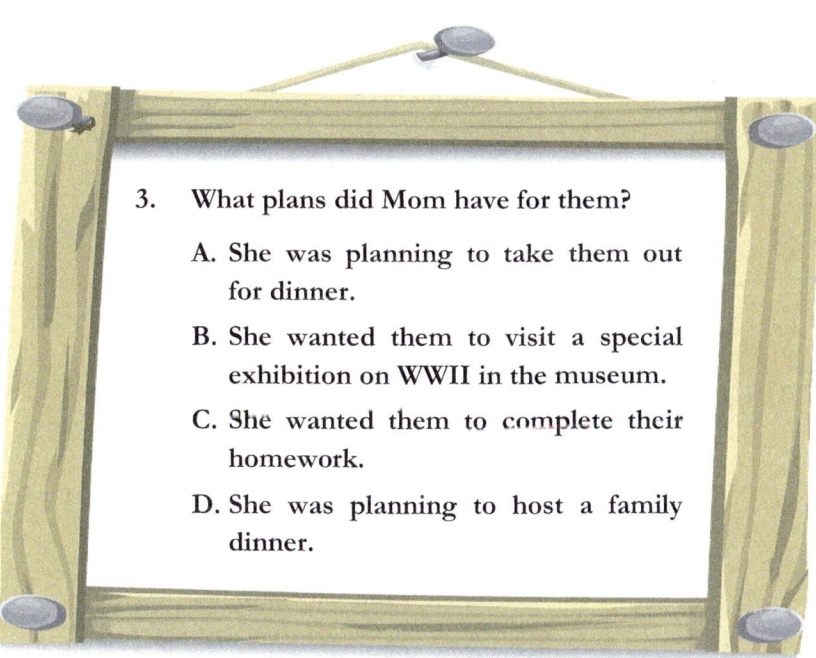

3. What plans did Mom have for them?

   A. She was planning to take them out for dinner.
   B. She wanted them to visit a special exhibition on WWII in the museum.
   C. She wanted them to complete their homework.
   D. She was planning to host a family dinner.

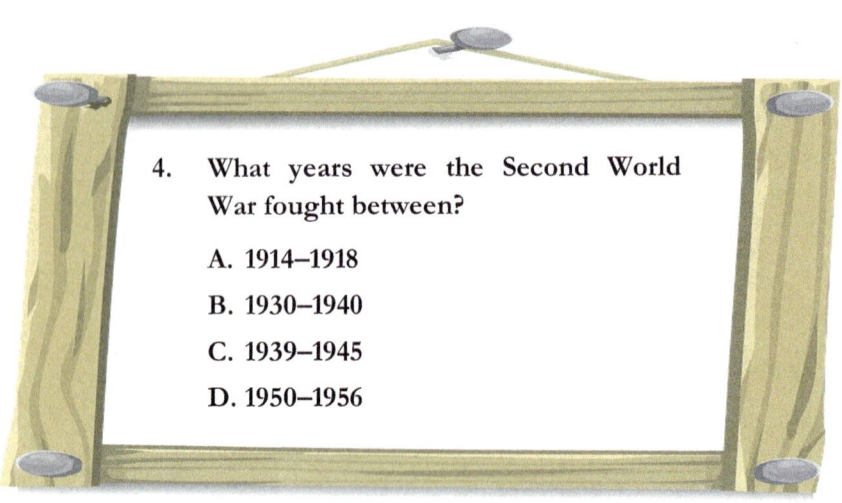

4. What years were the Second World War fought between?

   A. 1914–1918

   B. 1930–1940

   C. 1939–1945

   D. 1950–1956

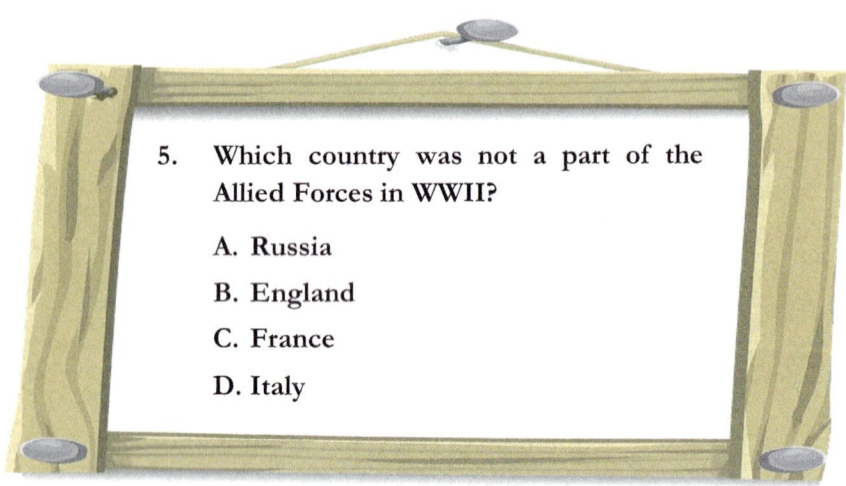

5. Which country was not a part of the Allied Forces in WWII?

   A. Russia

   B. England

   C. France

   D. Italy

Chapter 2:

The Time Travel Twist

What Could the Note Mean?

Tim voiced his thoughts first, "I think this means that for every winding of the clock, we will go 10 years into the past, right?"

Maya replied in a slow but serious way, "Yes, that's what it seems like."

Tim, not one to wait, plunged right in, "Let's go to the 1940s in London and see what the war looked like. Wouldn't that be fun?"

Maya was excited but said, "But what if it doesn't work? Worse, what if we get stuck there and can't come make it back? What if—"

Tim caught her arm, dragged her closer to the clock, and said, "Well, only one way to find out. Shall we?"

13

Despite her fear, Maya was just as adventurous as her brother. She nodded twice quickly. Tim started giving the huge key on the clockface one twist to the left after the next. After the eighth turn, Tim got a little confused because, in his excitement, he hadn't counted properly. After eight and a half turns backward, Tim whispered loudly, "London."

Only One Way to Find Out

For a moment, nothing happened, and Tim and Maya started to think it might all be a joke when suddenly they started to hear a swishing sound. It got louder and louder until they felt themselves being lifted and hurtled through a dark tunnel. The room had vanished around them. After what seemed like a minute or two, they landed on their feet with a thud on a hard floor.

They slowly opened their eyes to take in their surroundings. With a pang of disappointment, they realized it was the same old, dusty room! They could have sworn they had been flying, but now it looked like they just dreamed it all! What a letdown!

But as they listened carefully, they heard loud swooshing and bursts from somewhere above. It could have been above the building they were in. Who could be bursting firecrackers at this time of the day, and for what? Memorial Day was still another two days away!

They slowly walked toward the door of the room. As they pushed it open, there was a surprise. This wasn't the museum! This looked like a factory storage room. Why was everything so dark? The sound of fireworks, thunder, or whatever it was, was now deafening. What was happening? Where were they? Where was the home city they knew so well?

With pounding hearts, Tim and Maya managed to run out of the building into a deserted, dark street that looked nothing like the ones they knew. The road was cobbled for one thing. Every now and then, they came across buildings that seemed to have collapsed and were in shambles. This was not New York with its shiny tall skyscrapers!

Had a great fire swept through this city? Tim and Maya wondered.

Thankfully, soon, they saw another person coming their way. Through the foggy shadows, they noticed it was a boy, only a little taller and maybe older than Tim.

The boy was eyeing them strangely. Tim called out to him, "Hey there! Help! Where are we? What's happening?"

The boy ran up to them and said, "Hi there. I'm Thomas. Who are you? It's curfew time. You shouldn't be out during the Blackout."

Tim was wondering where he had heard Thomas's accent before. It was clear enough to understand but sounded different from how he or Maya spoke. Thomas's clothes also looked funny. He wore shorts and a shirt tucked in, with a long coat over it. He wore his socks pulled up over his calves and a pair of brown lace shoes on his feet. Thomas, in turn, was staring at Tim's brown pant, and button-up shirt.

Tim said, "I'm Tim, and this is my younger sister, Maya. We came over from America to meet relatives here. But we seem to have lost our parents on the way."

Thomas said, "Well, if we stay out here, we'll get hit by one of 'em German bombs! Quick, follow me; I'll take you to a shelter."

As they followed Thomas, it dawned on Tim that the boy looked like Tintin, the famous cartoon detective. Tim used to watch the show on TV when he was younger.

"Tintin was created in the 1920s," Dad had explained, "and that's why the characters are dressed in a different style." Thomas's shorts and jacket looked old-fashioned.

Maya placed the accent. Thomas spoke a little like the characters in *Peppa Pig*, the cartoon she used to watch when she was 4 or 5. Their mom had explained once that British English had an accent that sounded different from American English.

When Maya told him this, Tim connected the dots and realized they must have gone back in time. He had never met a boy dressed so formally in the 2020s, unless it was a function or they were wearing a school uniform! Tim quickly whispered his findings to Maya. Thomas walked ahead of them, leading them. He anxiously looked up at the sky above now and then.

Maya nodded. She whispered back to Tim that they must be in London when the Germans were bombing it! Remembering what John, their guide at the museum, told them, Maya guessed the year must be 1940 or 1941.

They looked up together and just managed to spot the tail of a small aircraft flying high over them. They were about to see, hear, and experience the German attack—the Blitzkrieg! Their excitement was replaced by fear. They understood Thomas wasn't joking—their lives were in danger unless they moved fast!

Do You Know?

Barrage balloons were giant, round balloons with long fins on the back to keep them upright. The British set them up where important targets were located. The biggest balloons were almost 60 feet long—as long as a school bus. Their job was to block planes from flying low and getting too close to targets. The higher the German planes flew to avoid the balloons, the harder it was for them to hit their targets with bombs. These balloons not only prevented enemy crafts from getting too near but were also tied to the ground with strong metal cables that could damage or bring down a plane that flew into them. During the Blitz, over 100 German planes hit the cables of the barrage balloons, and about two out of every three of them crashed or had to land.

Key Words

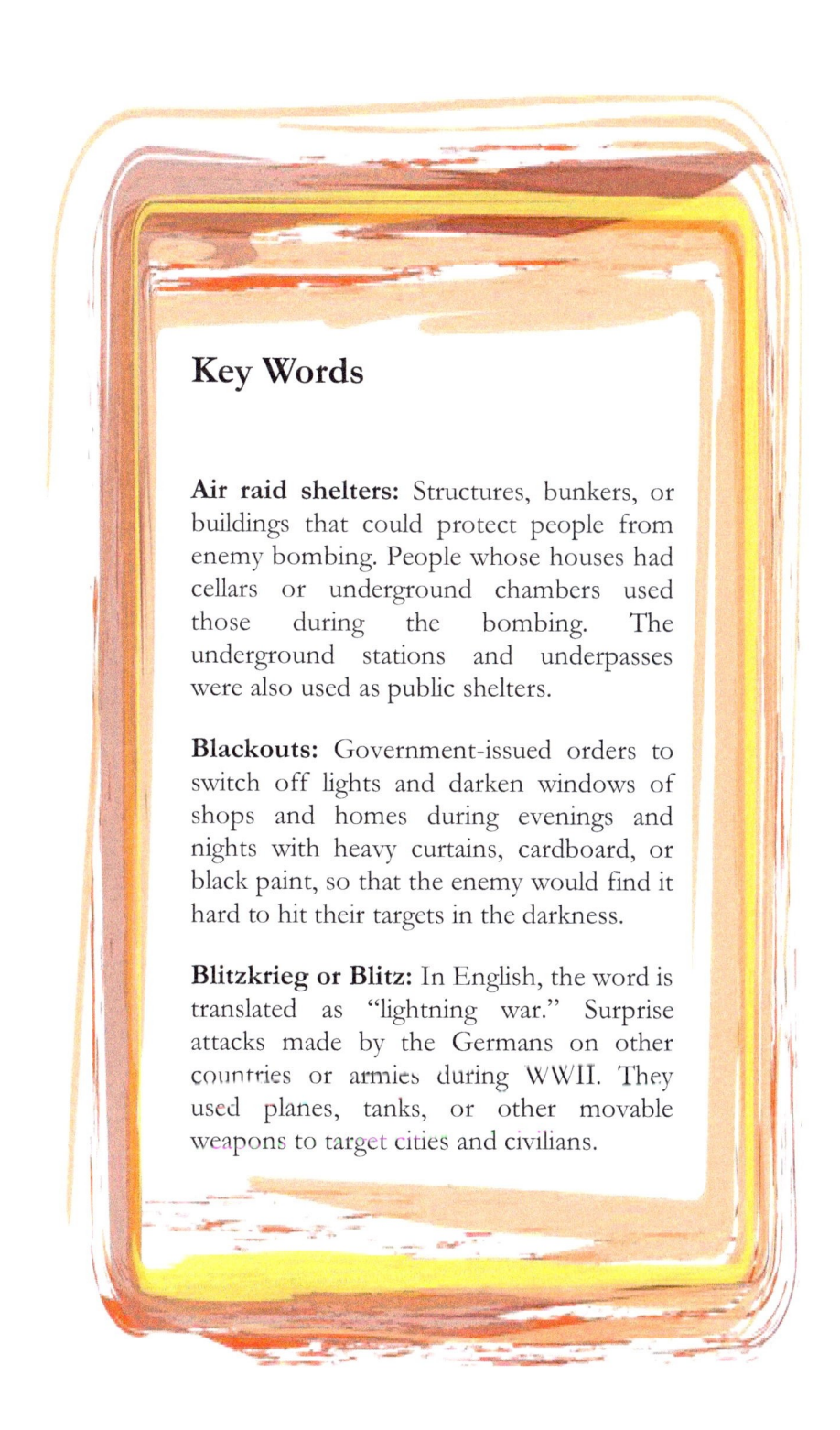

Air raid shelters: Structures, bunkers, or buildings that could protect people from enemy bombing. People whose houses had cellars or underground chambers used those during the bombing. The underground stations and underpasses were also used as public shelters.

Blackouts: Government-issued orders to switch off lights and darken windows of shops and homes during evenings and nights with heavy curtains, cardboard, or black paint, so that the enemy would find it hard to hit their targets in the darkness.

Blitzkrieg or Blitz: In English, the word is translated as "lightning war." Surprise attacks made by the Germans on other countries or armies during WWII. They used planes, tanks, or other movable weapons to target cities and civilians.

Curfew: A time given by the government by which people should be indoors. During WWII, lights were dimmed, shops closed, and people were asked to move to shelters or safe areas by 10:30 p.m. because the enemy bombed the city mostly at night.

Quiz

1. Why did Tim give the clock key eight and a half twists to the left?

    A. They wanted to travel 85 years into the past.

    B. They wanted to make the clock stop working.

    C. Tim wanted to play with the clock.

    D. Tim was confused about how many twists to give.

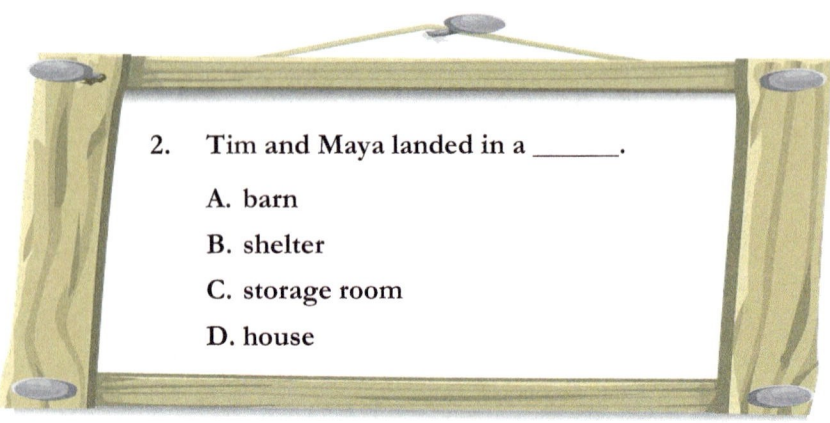

2. Tim and Maya landed in a _____.

   A. barn
   B. shelter
   C. storage room
   D. house

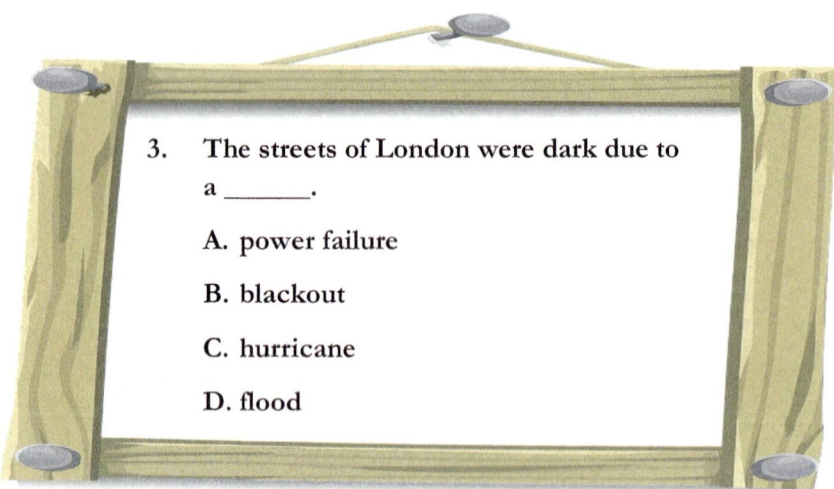

3. The streets of London were dark due to a _____.

   A. power failure
   B. blackout
   C. hurricane
   D. flood

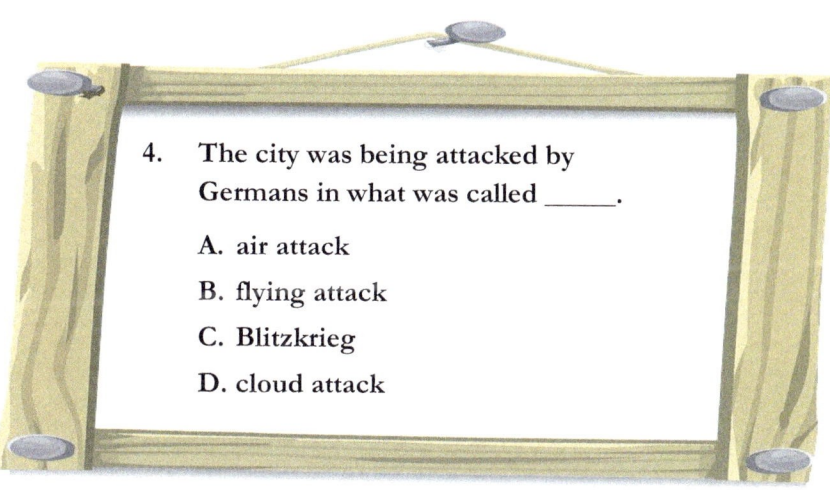

4. The city was being attacked by Germans in what was called _____.

   A. air attack
   B. flying attack
   C. Blitzkrieg
   D. cloud attack

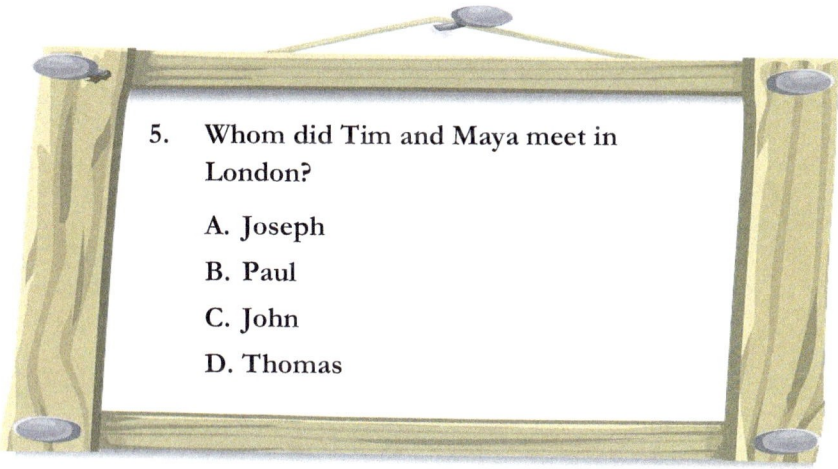

5. Whom did Tim and Maya meet in London?

   A. Joseph
   B. Paul
   C. John
   D. Thomas

Chapter 3:

The Blitz Experience

London, 1940

Thankfully, Thomas seemed a quiet sort and did not press them for details though he looked at their clothes and shoes quizzically. Tim knew it would do no good to say that he and Maya were from 85 years in the future. Thomas would probably think them mad. It was best to play along and learn more without revealing too much about who they were.

Thomas guided them to a little house by the end of the street and told them, "Go on inside, my family is there." He pointed to what looked like a little mud hut beside a brick house.

Tim couldn't stop himself from asking, "What is this? I've never seen anything like this."

Thomas said, "Wherever are you from!? You talk funny too—your English is a bit off, you know? Anyway, this is an Anderson Shelter. The government had us build it right before the war started. It's made from steel sheets, covered in mud on the outside, and buried halfway into the garden. This is our best bet against the German bombing. Of course, richer folks have their cellars and basements, but our house is modest. Every night, before the bombing begins, people like us crawl into these shelters and stay here till morning. The Luftwaffe doesn't bomb in daylight because they know the Royal air force will spot and take them down."

Tim suddenly understood. He chose to ignore Thomas's remarks about his accent and clothes. How could he explain what he, an American from the 21st century, was doing here in London in the 1940s?

Tim and Maya crept into the shelter and found inside a man, a lady, and a little girl. There were four bunkers built into the walls of the shelter. The little girl was in the smallest bunker, clutching her teddy bear to her chest, fast asleep. The man and woman got up as Thomas entered and introduced Tim and Maya to them.

He turned to them and said, "Tim and Maya, these are my parents, Mrs. and Mr. Hampton. That's my little sister, Flora."

Maya said, "Good evening, folks. We're so sorry to have bothered you. We came to the city last night but got separated from our parents."

Tim was glad Maya was a quick thinker.

Mr. Hampton said, "That's all right, kids. Thankfully, these shelters are built for six people, and you can stay here for the night till the bombing is over. Tomorrow, we'll figure out what to do."

Mrs. Hampton asked them, "Have you eaten? I have some bread and eggs left over from dinner."

The kids were not particularly hungry but took the food so their actions would match their story. After the first mouthful, they could not eat it. The bread was hard and dry, and the eggs tasted funny.

Mrs. Hampton sighed, "Scrambled eggs, made from the dried egg powder never taste as good. Bread is also getting scarcer by the day. Hopefully, the days when we can eat fresh food again won't be far off—when the war and rationing end."

Tim nodded and asked, "Why did it all start?"

How Did It All Start? What Can We Do?

Mr. Hampton said, "Well, it's simple, really. When the Great War ended in 1918, Germany was badly defeated and shamed by the rest of the world. Now that they have grown militarily strong under the dictatorship of Hitler and Nazi rule, they want their rightful place in world politics. When Germany invaded Poland in September 1939, Britain couldn't just watch on. France and our country jointly declared war on Germany almost immediately. But with the German Blitz or highly coordinated air and land attacks, France has fallen to the Nazis. Only the English Channel separates us from enemy territory now. That's why every last Brit will fight to the teeth to ensure our land remains free."

Tim and Maya started having a better idea of how things stood. They had many more doubts but couldn't risk asking all of them for fear of being caught out.

Maya asked, "But how can the public fight? Without weapons, aren't we all powerless?"

Thomas spoke, "We can do our bit. Small, individual, but united efforts can make a huge difference. Every evening, we stay indoors and ensure no light escapes our homes. We want the Germans to work in the dark and make mistakes so the British forces can shoot them down. We carry gas masks, which the government has issued us, at all times so that we can protect ourselves in case the Germans drop poison bombs on us."

Thomas's mother continued, "The rationing ensures all citizens have enough to eat. The government is also asking us to grow our own "Victory Gardens" through the "Dig for Victory" advertisements. In other words, many families, including ours, grow our vegetables and fruits in our backyards, so the country is well-fed. Doing our own work also gives us a purpose during these times. Many people work in factories, which helps the government focus its efforts on the production of arms and weapons we will need to fight the Germans."

What Next?

As they retired for the night, Tim and Maya were given two blankets and spare mattresses to sleep on the floor of the shelter.

It was Maya who first discovered a letter in her pocket. When he checked, Tim had the same in his pocket too. It looked like a continuation of the parchment paper they found in the clock. The letters said

> *The magic of the clock will run out. Use it wisely to visit places of your choice. Before this paper vanishes, wish yourself back home, to not get stuck where you are.*

It was true! Even as they looked at it, the letter was beginning to vanish slowly. If they didn't hurry, they wouldn't be able to see how World War II affected other places around the globe!

Tim and Maya decided they would stay back a little while more because Maya wanted to know more about how Britain responded to the Blitz and won the war.

Of course, they couldn't tell Thomas and his family about the victory, as that would give away who they were and where they were from!

Do You Know?

- The Coventry Blitz was the strongest attack by the Germans on the British during the German Operation Moonlight Sonata on November 14–15, 1940. Coventry Cathedral, dedicated to St. Michael, was destroyed, and King George VI is rumored to have cried when he saw the ruins the next day. The market square in Coventry and many houses were damaged. One man later remembered seeing hot, bubbling butter spilling out from a dairy nearby. The British motorcar manufacturing factory, Daimler, and its workshops in Coventry caught fire and were destroyed too. More than 550 people were officially reported killed in the air raids, though the numbers could have been much more.

- During the Blitz, 43,000 civilians lost their lives in the country, and London witnessed a massive loss of property. But the Germans miscalculated. They meant to wear out the morale of the citizens and get them to urge their government to surrender, but the British people became more united in their effort to fight the Germans. The public slogan was "Business as usual," as people were determined to keep calm and carry on as usual.

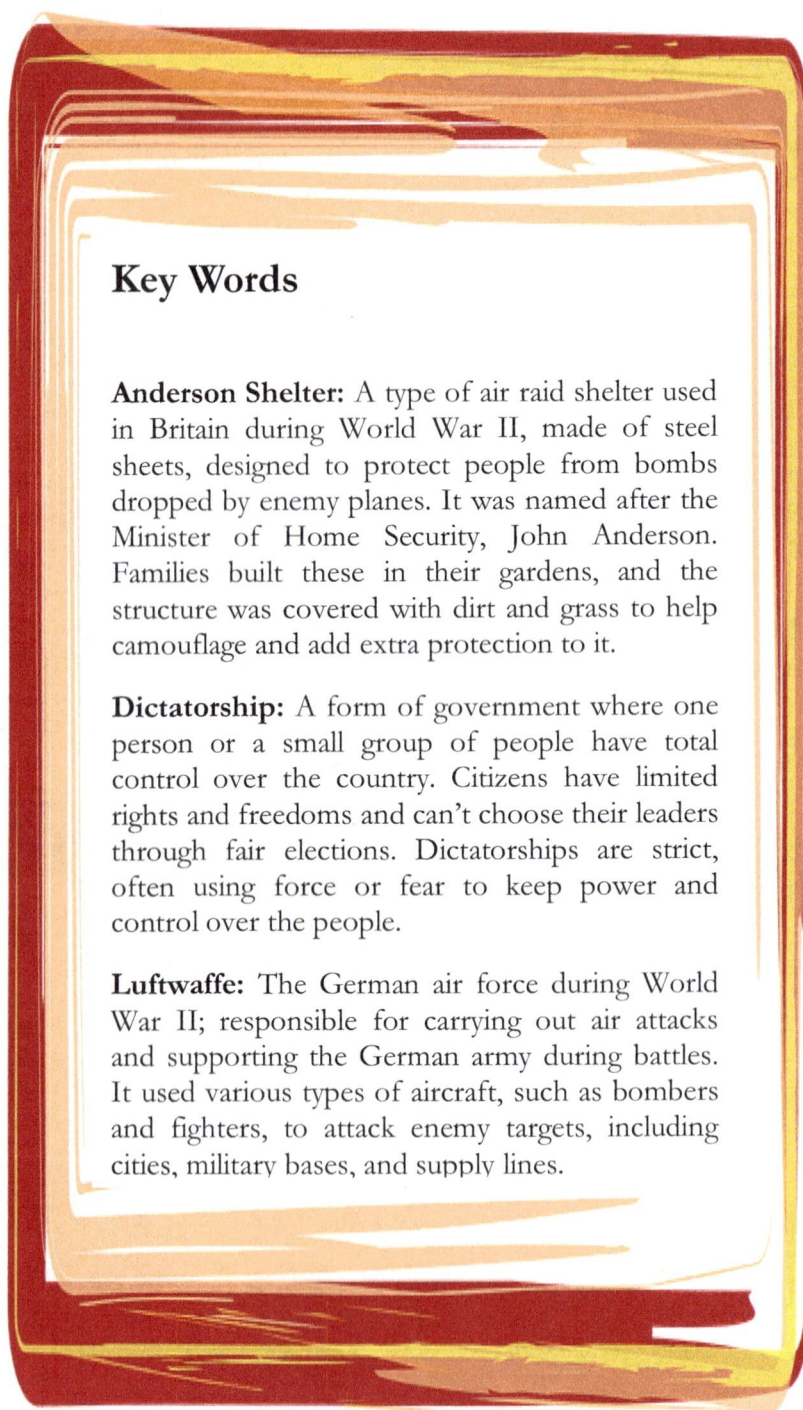

Key Words

Anderson Shelter: A type of air raid shelter used in Britain during World War II, made of steel sheets, designed to protect people from bombs dropped by enemy planes. It was named after the Minister of Home Security, John Anderson. Families built these in their gardens, and the structure was covered with dirt and grass to help camouflage and add extra protection to it.

Dictatorship: A form of government where one person or a small group of people have total control over the country. Citizens have limited rights and freedoms and can't choose their leaders through fair elections. Dictatorships are strict, often using force or fear to keep power and control over the people.

Luftwaffe: The German air force during World War II; responsible for carrying out air attacks and supporting the German army during battles. It used various types of aircraft, such as bombers and fighters, to attack enemy targets, including cities, military bases, and supply lines.

Rationing: A government-controlled way to save food and other important resources during the war and to ensure everyone got a fair share. In the UK, people could only buy a limited quantity of sugar, meat, butter, clothes, gas, and other items monthly, based on coupons in the ration books given to them.

Quiz

1. What was built outside Thomas's house to protect the family from air raids?

    A. An Anderson Shelter

    B. A Morrison Shelter

    C. A communal shelter

    D. An underground station

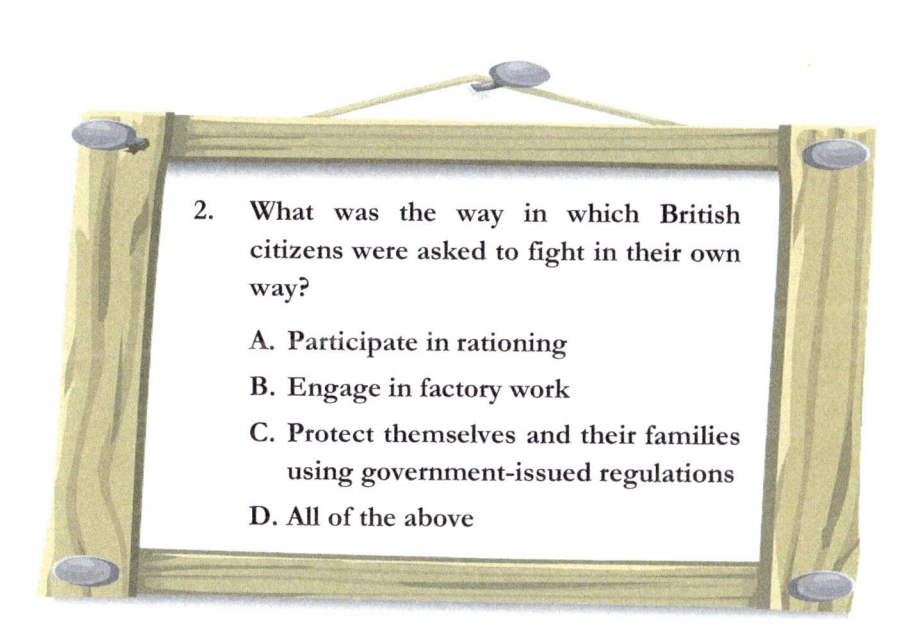

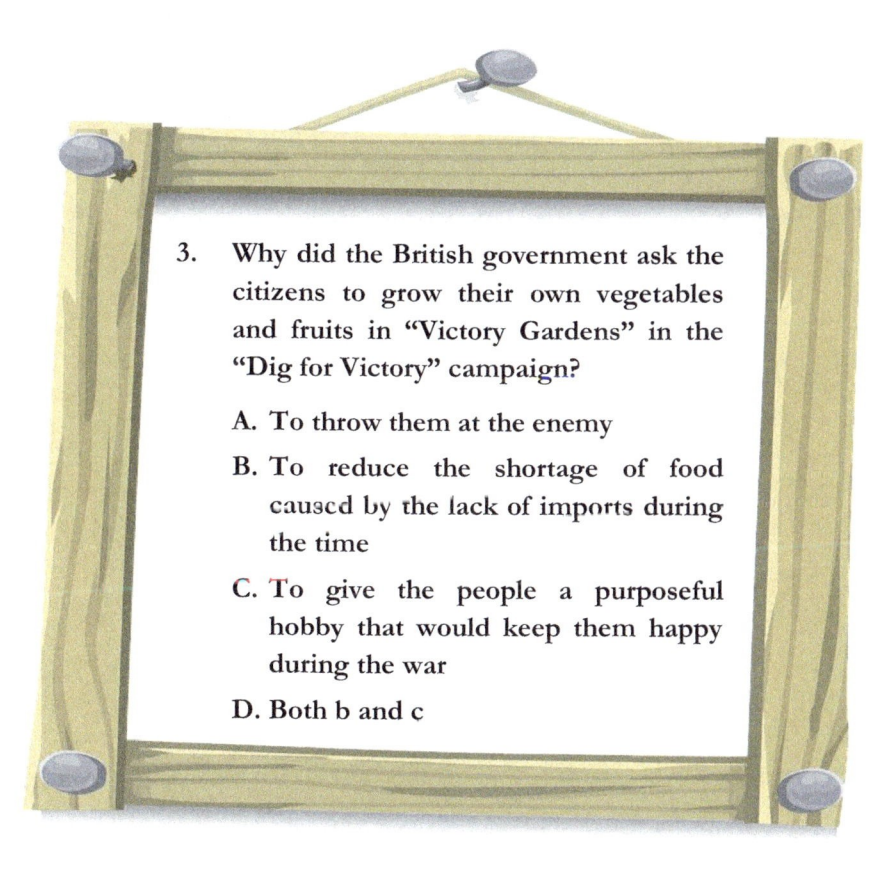

2. What was the way in which British citizens were asked to fight in their own way?

   A. Participate in rationing
   B. Engage in factory work
   C. Protect themselves and their families using government-issued regulations
   D. All of the above

3. Why did the British government ask the citizens to grow their own vegetables and fruits in "Victory Gardens" in the "Dig for Victory" campaign?

   A. To throw them at the enemy
   B. To reduce the shortage of food caused by the lack of imports during the time
   C. To give the people a purposeful hobby that would keep them happy during the war
   D. Both b and c

4. How did the Blackouts in the cities help?

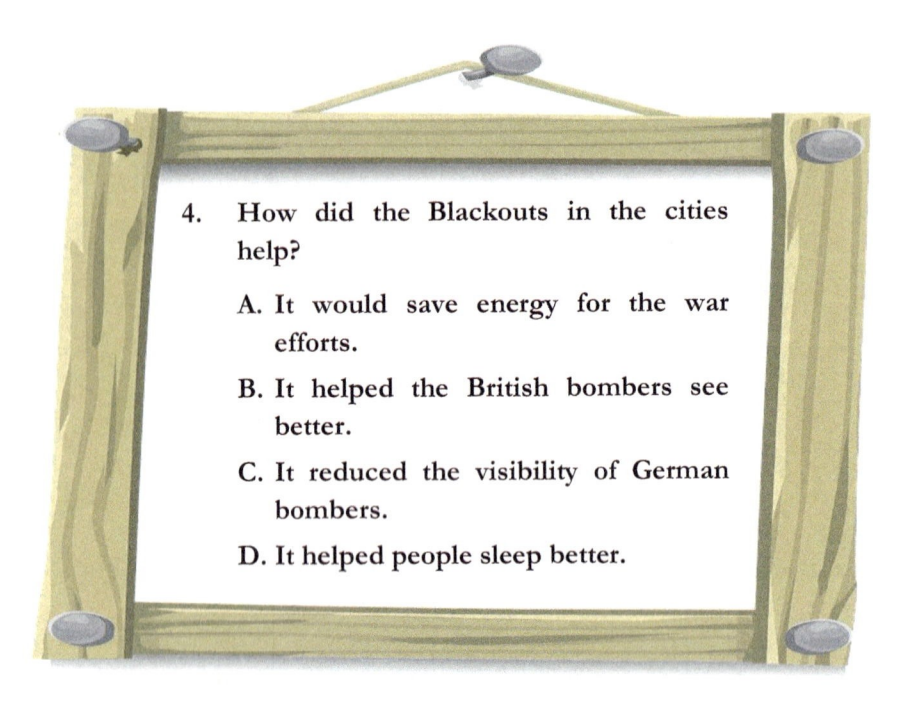

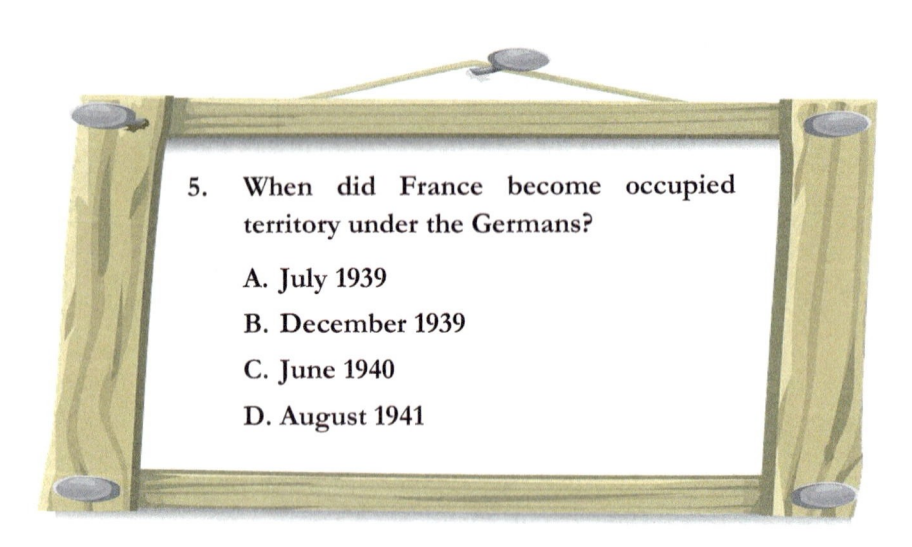

   A. It would save energy for the war efforts.

   B. It helped the British bombers see better.

   C. It reduced the visibility of German bombers.

   D. It helped people sleep better.

5. When did France become occupied territory under the Germans?

   A. July 1939

   B. December 1939

   C. June 1940

   D. August 1941

Chapter 4:

The Battle of Britain and Winston Churchill

The British Bulldog

Tim and Maya woke up early the next day. The deafening silence after the air raids made them feel unsettled. As they got up wondering what to do and where to go next, Thomas called them for breakfast. All of them trooped back into the house.

They got to know 6-year-old Flora better. She loved her toys, and nothing seemed to upset her much. She seemed to take the war as a natural event happening around her.

Tim and Maya now had an opportunity to look around Thomas's house. It was small and homey, with a living room, kitchen, dining room, and three bedrooms. Tim and Maya noted with surprise that there weren't any labor-saving appliances like a fridge, vacuum, or washing machine. This meant that sweeping had to be done with a broom and dustpan, clothes washed by hand, and food specially prepared to be preserved or finished the day it was cooked. It seemed like a hard life, especially with the war happening. In the living room, the central places were occupied by an old radio called a wireless set, a record player, and a fireplace. They had only seen models and photos of the radio and record player. What a far cry it was from the TV, smartphone, tablet, and other devices they had at home!

The whole family went about their daily chores quickly and efficiently. After all, government ads always reminded the public that the country had to go about their "business as usual" to help keep the enemy away! Children usually still had school, unless they were told not to come. Fathers often left for work as usual and mothers ensured homes ran as smoothly as possible. However, today, the family was gathered around the radio where Prime Minister Winston Churchill's speech was being broadcast.

As they gathered and waited, Tim wanted to know what Thomas liked best about the British prime minister. Thomas couldn't stop talking about the great man, who, he was sure, would lead their nation to victory. He told them that Churchill was already 65 years old when he came into the position but that he was the very image of the British fighting spirit. This was probably why he was fondly called "the British Bulldog." Thomas also told Tim and Maya that while politicians like Neville Chamberlain, the prime minister before Churchill, had tried unsuccessfully to pacify Germany and prevent a war with them, Churchill went all out and bravely spoke out against the Nazis.

Vaguely, Tim and Maya remembered that Winston Churchill was best known for his fierce, patriotic speeches that kept up the spirit of the tired English public throughout the war. They couldn't wait to hear his speech in real time!

The Battle of Britain—Aerial Warfare

Despite the poor transmission quality of the wireless set, the words of the Prime Minister rang out, powerful and moving. He called for "every man and woman" to prepare to do their duties "with special pride and care" (Churchill, 1940).

He reminded people that starting September 5, 1940, the German air force had started attacking cities like London instead of just military bases. He promised to keep fighting for victory and told them how even though the Germans were attacking, British fighter planes were stopping them, and the enemy was losing more planes and pilots than Britain.

Churchill warned the public that the Germans were preparing to invade their country by gathering ships and troops nearby, comparing this moment in history to famous battles in the past that England had withstood. He encouraged everyone to be ready to defend their country, emphasizing that while British forces were strong, the support of the Home Guard, made up of everyday citizens, was essential to their success.

Even though the Germans were trying to scare the people by bombing cities, Churchill said that the British spirit would remain unconquerable and that they would eventually defeat the enemy. He praised the brave efforts of Londoners during the bombings and ended with a message of hope for the British soldiers, stating that they would continue to fight for a better future.

Thomas clapped after the speech, and Mr. Hampton said the Battle of Britain would definitely be won, even if the British had to fight their way through hardships.

Maya asked, a little confused, "Is another battle coming?"

Mrs. Hampton smiled and said, "No, dear, this *is* the Battle of Britain. Mr. Churchill coined the name when the Germans started bombing the country in June, around the time France fell. At the time, the Nazis were destroying the factories and defense bases of our country mostly. But as you saw last night and have heard just now, the air raids on cities have started and will continue to target ordinary people. Our air force will fight back to defend this country until they are forced to turn back."

Mr. Hampton continued, "As Mr. Churchill warned us in his very first speech to the House of Commons as Prime Minister, the British are only going to see days of 'blood, toil, tears, and sweat.' But we have no choice. If our nation too, like Norway, Belgium, and France, falls into the hands of these evil men, then there is no knowing what dark ages the world will fall into."

Tim and Maya nodded gravely.

Do You Know?

- Royal Air Force Sergeant Ray Holmes saw a German bomber flying towards Buckingham Palace on September 15, 1940. He had used all his bullets in a previous fight and decided to keep going. He flew his plane, a Hawker Hurricane, straight at the German bomber, a Dornier, and crashed into it with his wing. This knocked off the bomber's tail and it crashed down into Victoria Tube Station. Though his plane was damaged, Holmes was able to jump out using his parachute and land, hanging from the roof of a nearby apartment building. This incredible event was partly filmed and people celebrated Holmes as a national hero for protecting the royal palace from danger.

- The British officially recorded the duration of the Battle of Britain as being from July 10–October 31, 1940, which overlaps the period of the Blitz, from September 7, 1940, to May 11, 1941. German historians regard the battle as a single campaign lasting from July 1940 to May 1941, a timeline including the Blitz. In either case, the outcome remains the same—England's victory in successfully defending itself from a German invasion.

Key Words

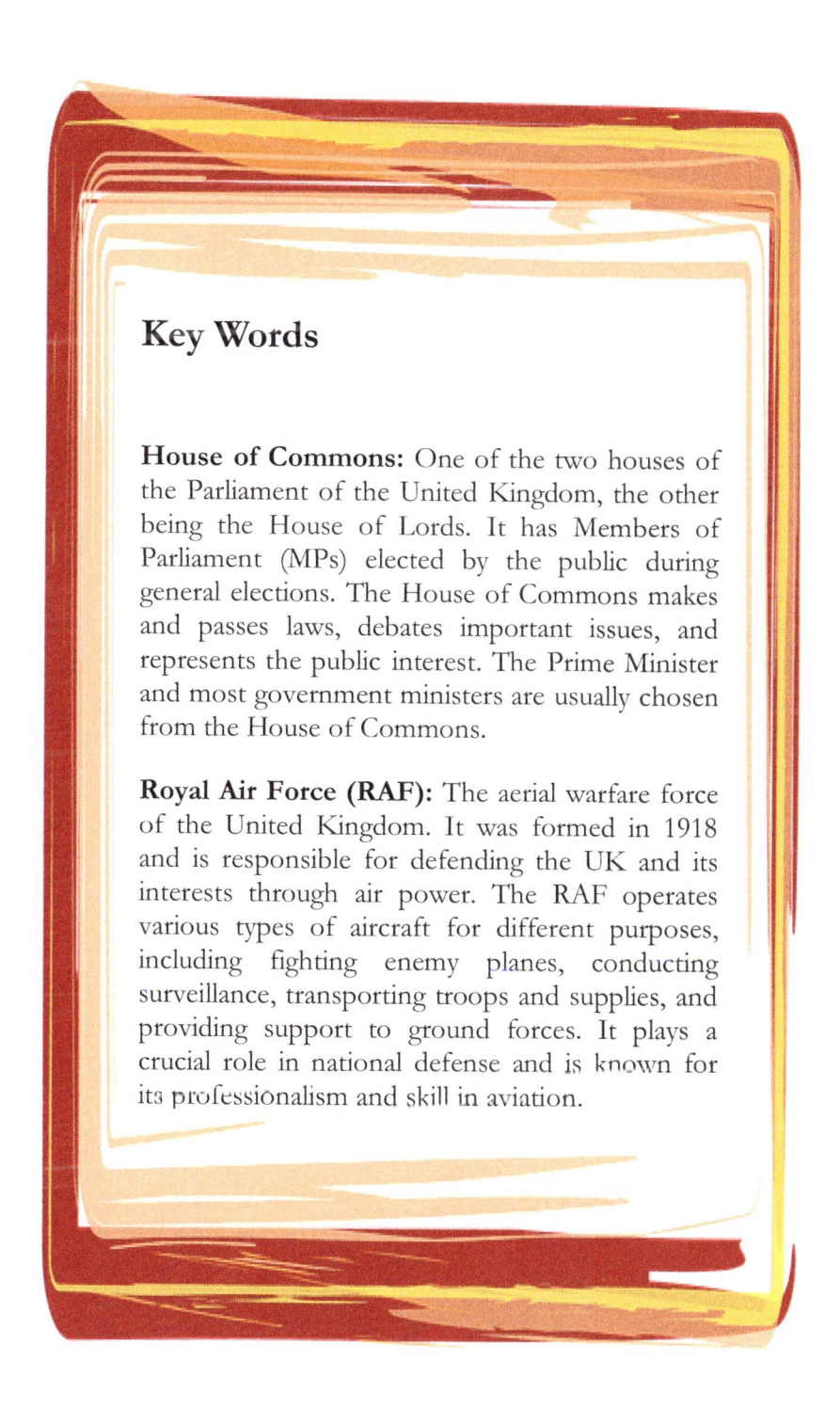

House of Commons: One of the two houses of the Parliament of the United Kingdom, the other being the House of Lords. It has Members of Parliament (MPs) elected by the public during general elections. The House of Commons makes and passes laws, debates important issues, and represents the public interest. The Prime Minister and most government ministers are usually chosen from the House of Commons.

Royal Air Force (RAF): The aerial warfare force of the United Kingdom. It was formed in 1918 and is responsible for defending the UK and its interests through air power. The RAF operates various types of aircraft for different purposes, including fighting enemy planes, conducting surveillance, transporting troops and supplies, and providing support to ground forces. It plays a crucial role in national defense and is known for its professionalism and skill in aviation.

Wireless: Crucial for military operations, the most common wireless system used was the radio set, allowing leaders to talk to their people. Other forms of wireless communication used on the battlefield were CR100s, WS28s, and handie-talkies (or walkie-talkies), all of which used radio signals to allow real-time communication between soldiers.

Quiz

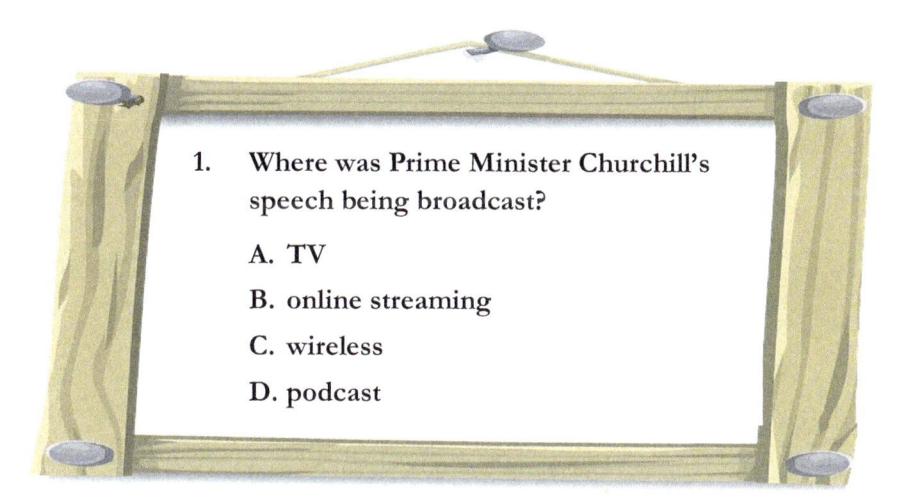

1. Where was Prime Minister Churchill's speech being broadcast?

   A. TV
   B. online streaming
   C. wireless
   D. podcast

2. Why was Churchill called the English Bulldog?

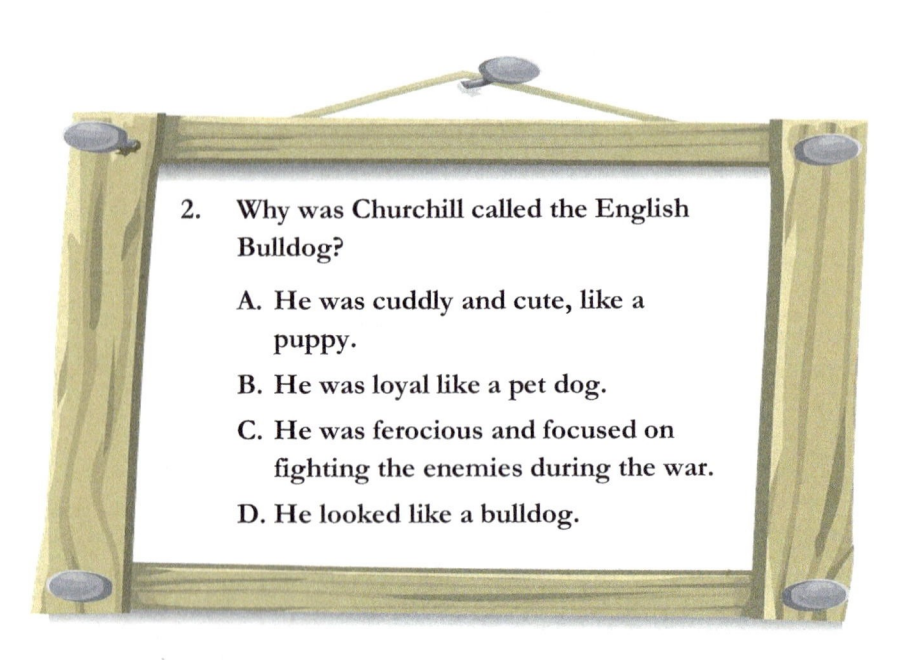

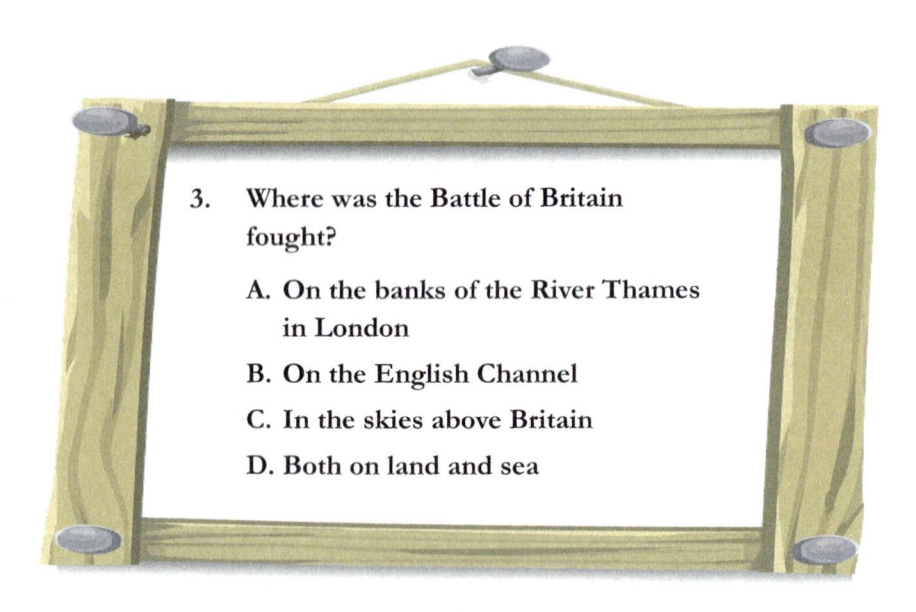

   A. He was cuddly and cute, like a puppy.
   B. He was loyal like a pet dog.
   C. He was ferocious and focused on fighting the enemies during the war.
   D. He looked like a bulldog.

3. Where was the Battle of Britain fought?

   A. On the banks of the River Thames in London
   B. On the English Channel
   C. In the skies above Britain
   D. Both on land and sea

4. What is Churchill remembered most for today?

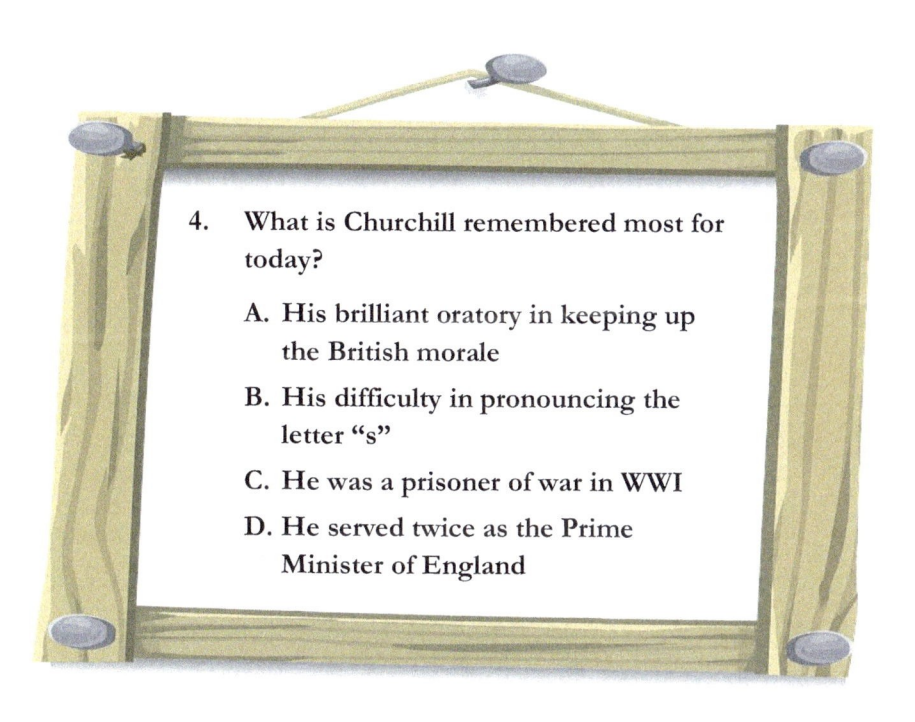

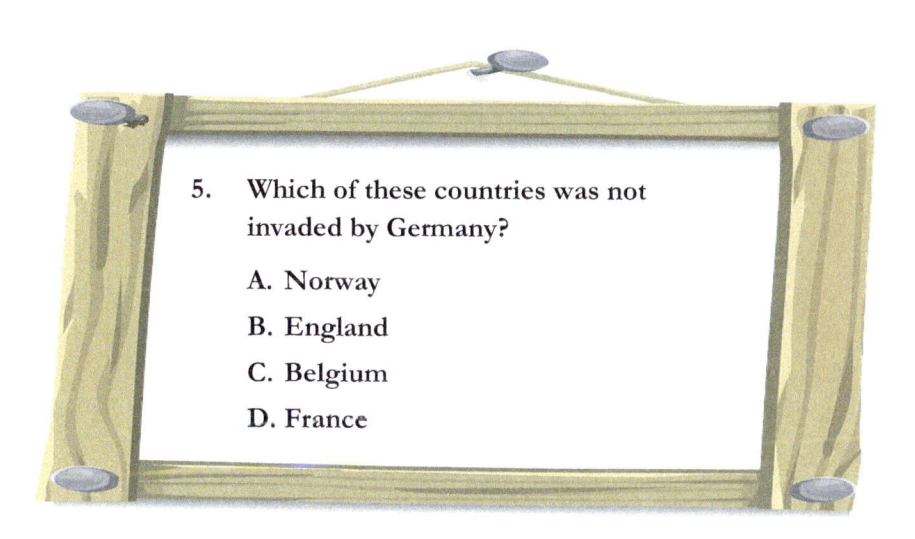

   A. His brilliant oratory in keeping up the British morale
   B. His difficulty in pronouncing the letter "s"
   C. He was a prisoner of war in WWI
   D. He served twice as the Prime Minister of England

5. Which of these countries was not invaded by Germany?

   A. Norway
   B. England
   C. Belgium
   D. France

Chapter 5:

Spies and Codebreakers at Bletchley Park

Bletchley Park

Thomas had cryptically told them that day that they would visit a place where people were "helping the Allies win the war." Tim and Maya were very curious about where they were headed. They waited with bated breaths as Thomas's father drove them to what looked like a big country mansion. Tim and Maya looked at each other confused. How would being in this big house help the Allies?

Thomas's father told them, "Now, kids, what happens here is extremely important but top-secret work. We should be very careful not to disturb the people working. I have some work here, and you can look around."

The kids nodded at him, though Tim and Maya did not understand anything.

Thomas explained, "This is Bletchley Park in Milton Keynes, Buckinghamshire. This is where the spies on our side work, and we will be looking at some groundbreaking technology in reading the ciphers and codes of the enemy."

Suddenly Maya looked very interested. She loved word puzzles and crosswords. She had heard of the Bletchley Circle of Codebreakers, who played a major part in the Allied victory. She couldn't wait to meet them and learn more about their work.

She asked, "But how do they work here escaping detection? I mean, won't someone find out and reveal their location to the enemy?"

Thomas laughed, "Only a select few, including us now, know of their existence. There are other codebreakers working all over the country too. This delegation came here calling themselves Captain Ridley's Shooting Party in 1938, pretending to be a gathering for a country party. They were mainly part of the MI6 or the Secret Service. Dad says there are at least 150, if not more, people working here! Just before this war, they recruited professors from colleges, scientists, and even common people who loved to break crosswords and play chess to help break enemy codes. Come, let's go have a look. If we are lucky, we may even see Alan Turing at work."

Maya gasped. She had watched a documentary on the life of the great mathematician who helped develop a machine that mechanized codebreaking, making it easier and faster. She could not believe that she might meet him in person.

Station X

Inside, the country house stopped looking anything like a house. The space was divided into workstations where people—both men and women, some in uniforms while others looked like students or civilians, were working away at sheets of paper. On looking closer, the paper contained scribbled letters. They were the codes of enemy messages being broadcast by Morse code through radio signals. It was easy enough to convert the Morse into letters. The problem was that nobody knew what these letters meant. The Germans used a machine called the Enigma to code their messages. The machine had truly lived up to its name because the British still found it hard to break it, especially when the Germans kept changing the settings of the machine. Until the Allies understood all the secrets of the Enigma, the messages would remain meaningless alphabets and numbers.

Thomas said, "My dad told me that these people are called the Government Code and Cypher School or GC & CS, under the Secret Intelligence Service that looks into national security. Admiral Sir Hugh Sinclair, once the head of intelligence, helped set up this place. Unfortunately, he passed away two years ago from cancer. This station at Bletchley Park is codenamed Station X and the Germans have no clue that such a place even exists!"

Tim and Maya wondered if they would be able to have any real conversations with any of the people because all were just too busy! It was obvious that if the codebreakers did not figure out the codes in time, England would surely lose the war. These people were as important as the army, navy, and air force!

When a young girl, who must have been in her early 20s, bumped into Tim, she asked them, "Oh, sorry. Who are you?"

Thomas answered, "I am Mr. Hampton's son and these are my friends. My father works with Hut 8."

The girl smilingly said, "Oh, alright. I have a lot of work I must get back now," and darted off.

Maya asked, "What is a hut?"

Thomas said, "Since there are many enemy messages that come in from many places—some sent by their air force, some from their naval teams, and even from their army bases, our team is divided into huts that are numbered. Each hut works on encrypted messages from a particular place or source. The huts divide up the work."

Tim and Maya could see a complex network of information being gathered at Bletchley Park.

When they finally went in search of Mr. Hampton, they found him in Hut 8, a small wooden building outside the manor. He was in deep conversation with the famous Mr. Turing, who headed the operations of that hut.

Just in the Nick of Time

Mr. Hampton said, "Ah, Turing, just wanted to introduce my son, Thomas, and his friends who have joined me here today."

Turing smiled at them before getting back to his conversation with Mr. Hampton. Since the men were talking about technical and scientific details on how codes could be broken, the children understood very little. Maya observed how young Alan Turing seemed to be and how shy and humble he generally was. Yet, when he started talking about codes and math, he was very confident in himself.

A young cryptanalyst ran up to Turing and said, "Sir, this has just come in, and it seems to be very important, about an attack on our ships in the Pacific."

Alan Turing quickly gave orders for the message to be immediately run through the Bombe—the decoding machine that he himself had helped build. It was installed in Hut 1. A person ran out with the message as the team waited.

In a little while, a messenger arrived with the decoded message that Turing and Thomas's father read.

Finally, Turing said, "I think the Prime Minister will want to hear of this. Thank God, we received this Ultra now!" He went to place a secure call.

Thomas's father later explained that "Ultra" was the code word for high-level secret intelligence from the enemy.

When it was time for them to leave, Tim and Maya had a lot to think about.

Do You Know?

The Bletchley Park staff worked eight-hour shifts around the clock. However, it was not all work—The Bletchley Park Recreational Club included a drama group, library, music, dancing, games like bridge and chess, and sports like fencing.

Bletchley Park or Station X continued working after the Second World War. GC & CS left Bletchley Park in 1946 and moved to Eastcote, an earlier Bombe outstation in North West London, and later to Cheltenham, where it is still located today. Now it is known as the Government Communications Headquarters (GCHQ). The GCHQ's main building is known as the "Doughnut," because it is shaped like the beloved dessert.

Key Words

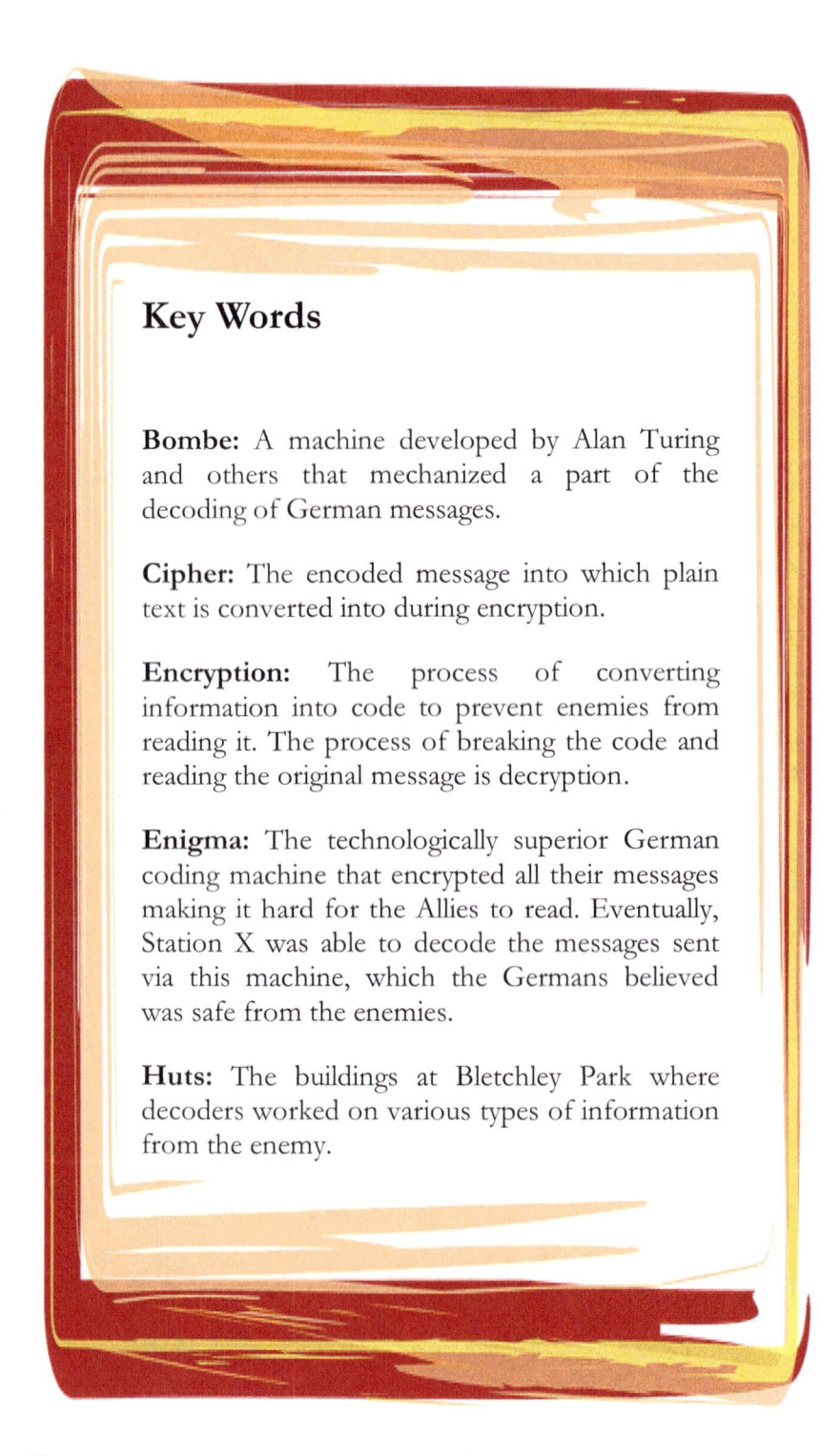

Bombe: A machine developed by Alan Turing and others that mechanized a part of the decoding of German messages.

Cipher: The encoded message into which plain text is converted into during encryption.

Encryption: The process of converting information into code to prevent enemies from reading it. The process of breaking the code and reading the original message is decryption.

Enigma: The technologically superior German coding machine that encrypted all their messages making it hard for the Allies to read. Eventually, Station X was able to decode the messages sent via this machine, which the Germans believed was safe from the enemies.

Huts: The buildings at Bletchley Park where decoders worked on various types of information from the enemy.

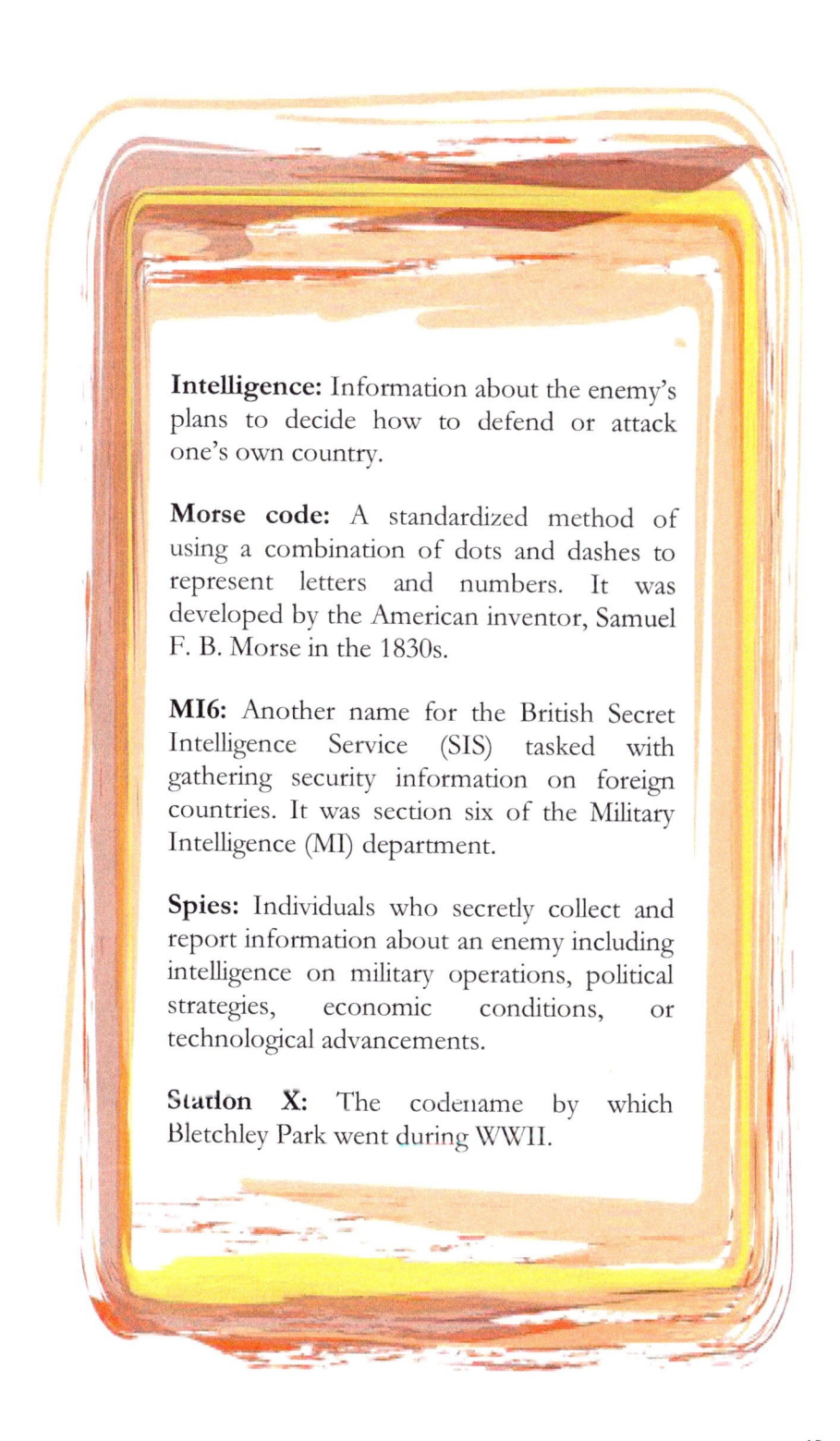

Intelligence: Information about the enemy's plans to decide how to defend or attack one's own country.

Morse code: A standardized method of using a combination of dots and dashes to represent letters and numbers. It was developed by the American inventor, Samuel F. B. Morse in the 1830s.

MI6: Another name for the British Secret Intelligence Service (SIS) tasked with gathering security information on foreign countries. It was section six of the Military Intelligence (MI) department.

Spies: Individuals who secretly collect and report information about an enemy including intelligence on military operations, political strategies, economic conditions, or technological advancements.

Station X: The codename by which Bletchley Park went during WWII.

Ultra: Important information gathered from German communications through their Enigma machines, which helped the Allies understand the German military plans and movements.

Quiz

1. How did the Germans send their messages and plans from one place to another?

   A. They sent coded messages using radio signals.

   B. They used telephones to call one another.

   C. They sent emails.

   D. They never sent any messages at all.

2. Why were there many huts at Bletchley Park?

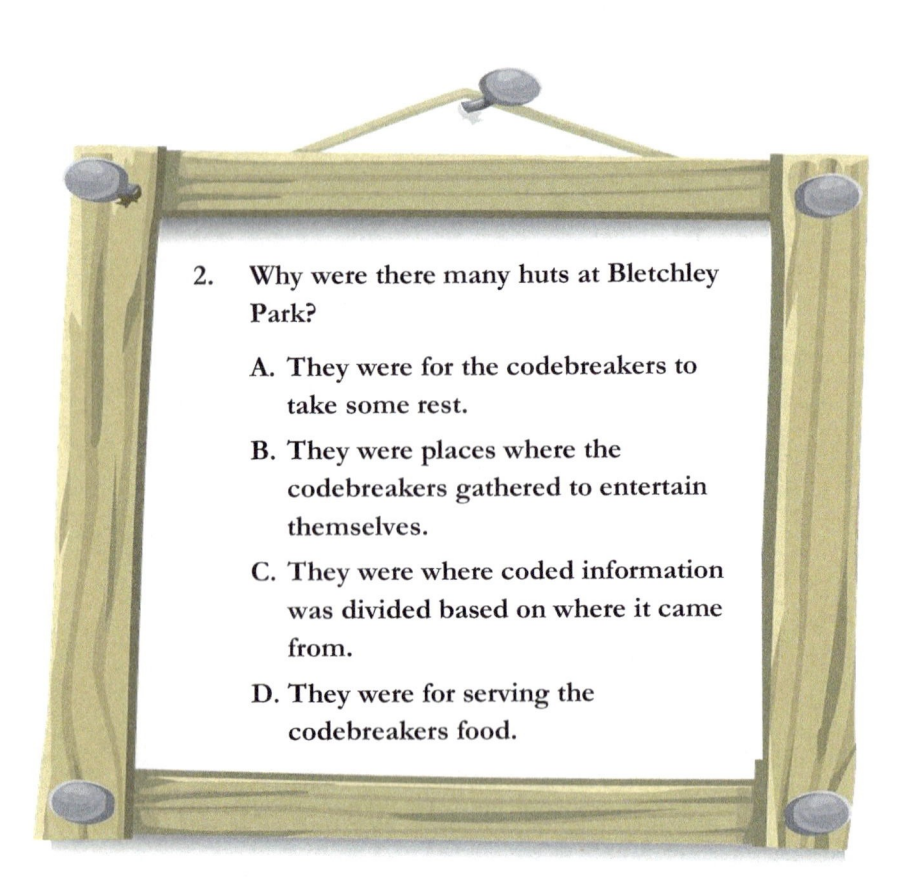

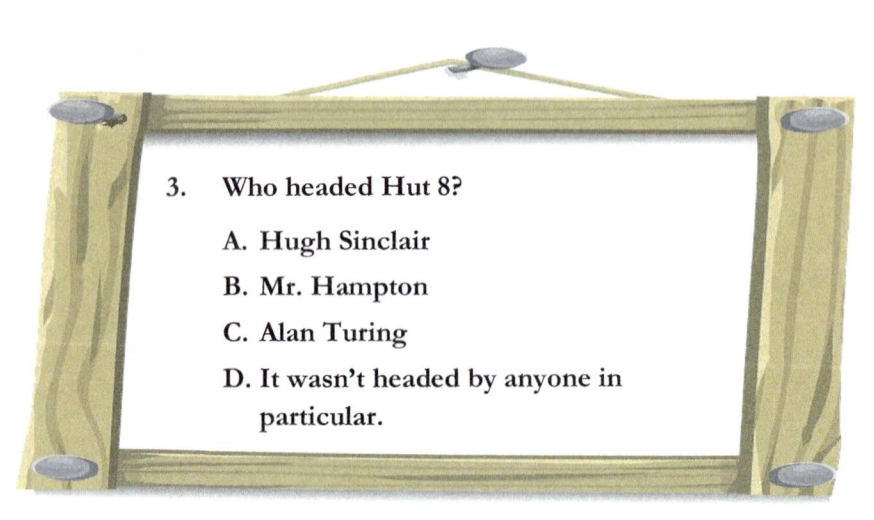

   A. They were for the codebreakers to take some rest.
   B. They were places where the codebreakers gathered to entertain themselves.
   C. They were where coded information was divided based on where it came from.
   D. They were for serving the codebreakers food.

3. Who headed Hut 8?

   A. Hugh Sinclair
   B. Mr. Hampton
   C. Alan Turing
   D. It wasn't headed by anyone in particular.

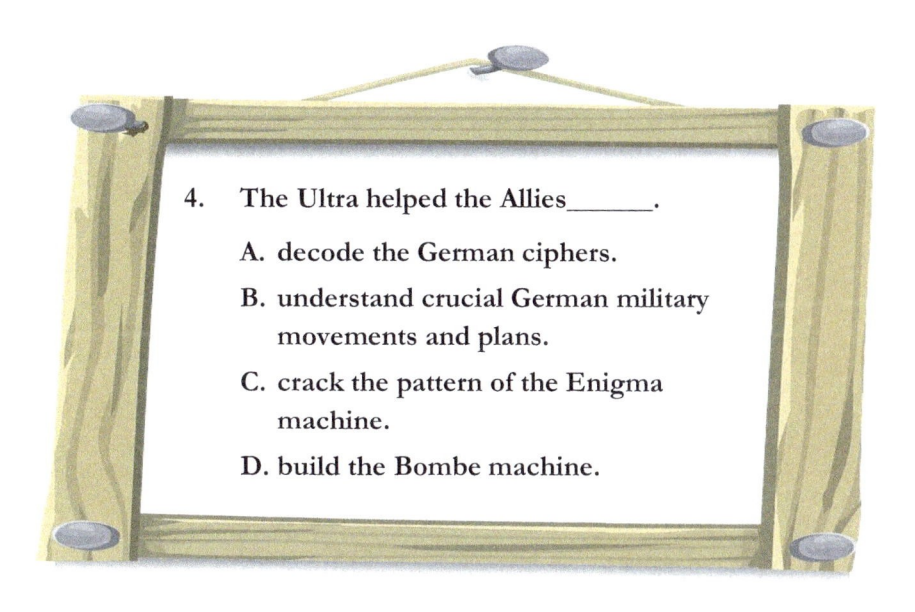

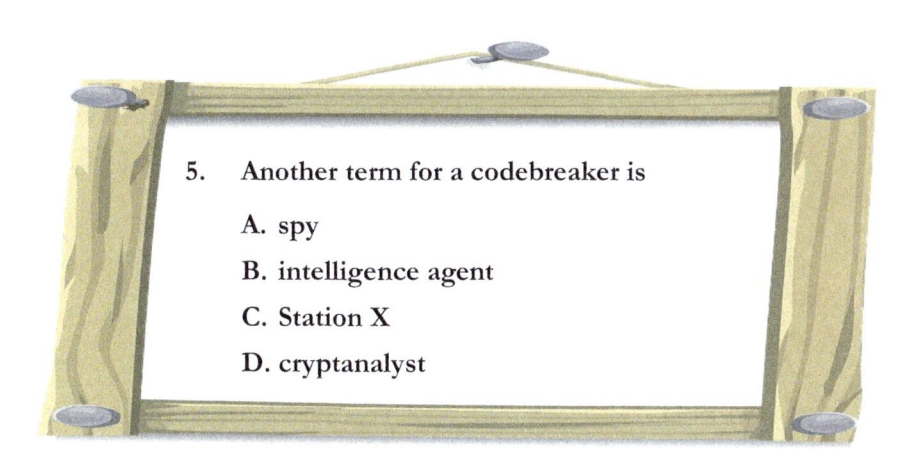

4. The Ultra helped the Allies_____.

   A. decode the German ciphers.
   B. understand crucial German military movements and plans.
   C. crack the pattern of the Enigma machine.
   D. build the Bombe machine.

5. Another term for a codebreaker is

   A. spy
   B. intelligence agent
   C. Station X
   D. cryptanalyst

Chapter 6:

Women at War

The Munitions Factory

On the way back to London, Mr. Hampton said there was a message he had to give at a munitions factory. These were also called Royal Ordnance Factories or ROFs, where arms and weapons for the war were being made. Tim was very happy as he loved to learn about war weapons and vehicles.

Mr. Hampton said that this particular factory made bombs, guns, shells, and cartridge cases and engaged people in the filling of explosives. They were going to the Royal Arsenal in Woolwich on the banks of the River Thames. The factory was also called Woolwich Warren because once upon a time, the lands here were used as a domestic warren, that is for the breeding and raising of rabbits.

The ordnance factory was located in what looked like a really old-fashioned house. Mr. Hampton told them that this was a house from the 16th century called Tower Place. It had belonged to a wealthy goldsmith and merchant who later became the Mayor of London. Afterward, the Office of Ordnance bought the place and used it for storing guns.

In the late 17th century, the storage unit slowly expanded to include a research wing where explosives and weapons were developed and tested. Initially, all the weapons were handmade. Little by little, the operations were mechanized so that different parts of the gun and explosives could be manufactured faster.

In the Great War, the arsenal had 80,000 workers and it never stopped working, even though some of the other weapon factories had been shut down after the war in 1918.

Women in the War

When they got there, Tim was surprised. He had expected to see only men. It was only when he saw them that he remembered how women also played a huge role in WWII. The women were dressed like the men—in brown overalls and wooden clogs that protected them from the chemicals, sharp objects, and sparks from the furnaces.

Maya was thrilled to see how women were working alongside men and helping to stack cartridges, make bullets, fill up explosives, and even operate heavy machines like cranes. Even in 2020s New York, she rarely saw a woman working in a factory or driving a heavy vehicle like a bus! The work in munitions factories was not easy. Mr. Hampton said many workers worked long hours, all seven days of the week. They were paid well, though the women were paid less than the men. Tim and Maya thought this was unfair. There was also the risk of getting injured by the machinery or chemicals used in explosives.

When Maya expressed her awe, Thomas said, "But this is not all. Women are everywhere. You have already met so many of them at

Bletchley Park. There is WRNS, the Woman's Navy; WAAF, the Women's Air Force; and even ATS, a division of the army for women. Do you know that our Prime Minister's daughter, Mary Churchill, and even the King's daughter, Princess Elizabeth are members of the ATS? Of course, the government still does not allow them into the battlefield to fight the enemy, but depending on their training, these women recruits are cooks, nurses, receptionists, drivers, or mechanics, and some of them can handle searchlights and anti-aircraft machinery. They do everything! Even the women at home have the duty of single-handedly managing homes and children while most of the men are away fighting. I feel women are doing much more than men!"

Tim and Maya had not thought of all these different roles the women were having to play during the war. Suddenly, they remembered their mother and felt a pang of sadness thinking how they always took her for granted and grumbled when she said things for their own good. They decided that when they got home, they would try to be better and help her more.

Tim and Maya faced a practical problem: Now, it was time for them to move on and learn more about the war in different places. They decided to learn about America's entry into WWII. They knew they would have to be at Pearl Harbor in December 1941 to do this.

Do You Know?

- WWII was not the first time women worked in factories During the First World War, women were employed too. Some of these women worked with an explosive, poisonous chemical called "TNT," which was used as the filling for shells. The human skin exposed to TNT becomes yellowish-orange in color. These girls, whose skins were always stained yellow from their work, were called "Canary Girls," reminding us of the yellow-orange feathers of the canary bird. Some of these women went on to have "canary babies" whose skins were also yellowish. Over time, when exposure to the chemical stopped, the color faded.

- Rosie the Riveter is an imaginary character based on real-life ammunition workers invented by America during WWII. Dressed in blue overalls, wearing a red polka-dotted head scarf, and holding a drill in her hand, Rosie often appeared on posters calling for women and encouraging them to work in the arms factories. These posters used to have the famous caption, "We can do it!"

- The Soviet Union was the first country to use female pilots in WWII. The "Night Witches" were a group of Soviet women led by fighter pilots like Marina Raskova, who were trained in air raids. During the night, they would cut off their engines to fly silently and drop bombs over German cities and targets. They did not use radios and were almost impossible to detect. The Germans would hear the whooshing sound of their planes, reminding them of sweeping brooms. This is what earned these women their nickname. The Germans feared and hated them so much that any airman who shot down a Night Witch was awarded the Iron Cross medal.

Key Words

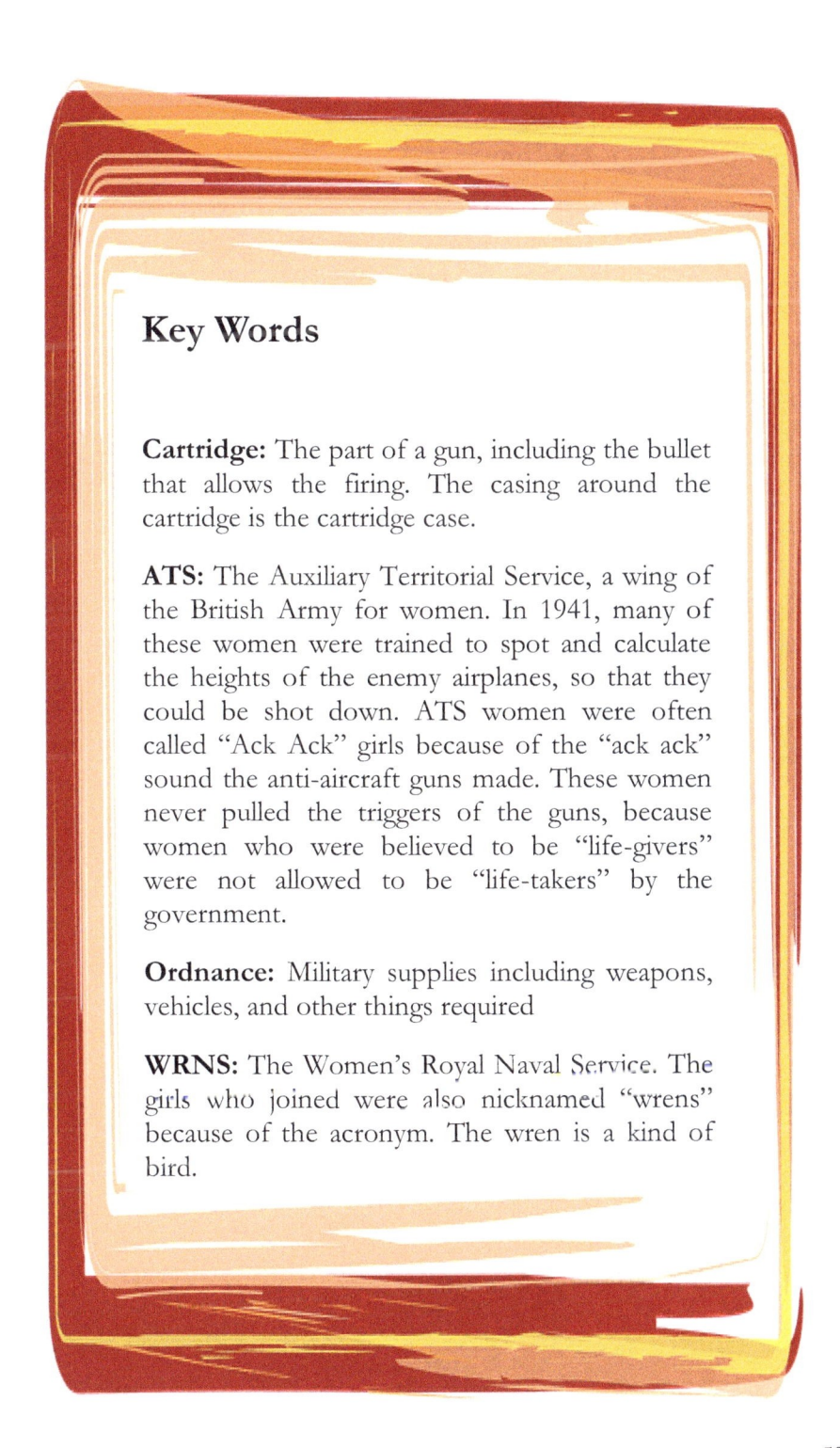

Cartridge: The part of a gun, including the bullet that allows the firing. The casing around the cartridge is the cartridge case.

ATS: The Auxiliary Territorial Service, a wing of the British Army for women. In 1941, many of these women were trained to spot and calculate the heights of the enemy airplanes, so that they could be shot down. ATS women were often called "Ack Ack" girls because of the "ack ack" sound the anti-aircraft guns made. These women never pulled the triggers of the guns, because women who were believed to be "life-givers" were not allowed to be "life-takers" by the government.

Ordnance: Military supplies including weapons, vehicles, and other things required

WRNS: The Women's Royal Naval Service. The girls who joined were also nicknamed "wrens" because of the acronym. The wren is a kind of bird.

WAAF: The Women's Auxiliary Air Force. The women joiners were sometimes referred to as "Waafs."

Recruits: Individuals who have recently joined an organization, here, the military.

TNT: Trinitrotoluene, a chemical explosive used in grenades and bombs.

Quiz

1. What were munitions factories?

    A. toy shops

    B. food manufacturing units

    C. paper making companies

    D. factories for making weapons and arms

2. Woolwich was on the bank of River _____.

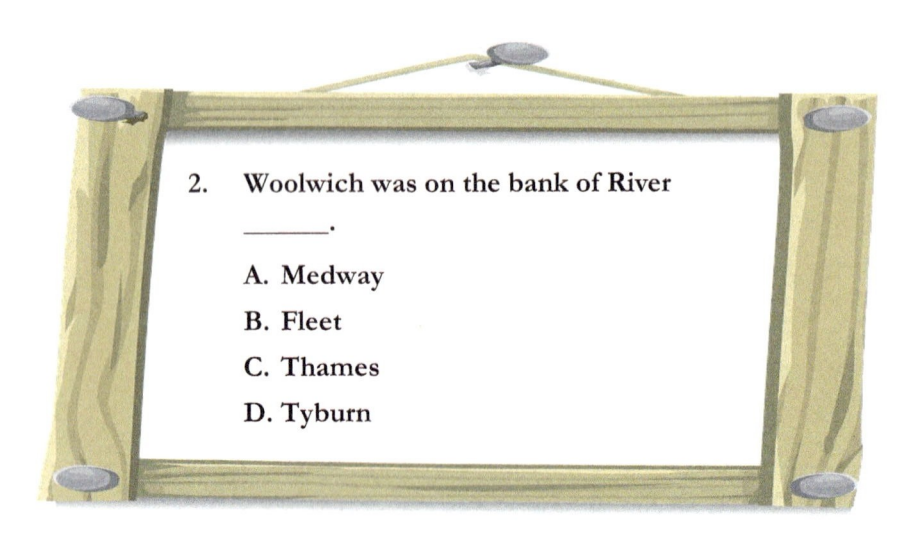

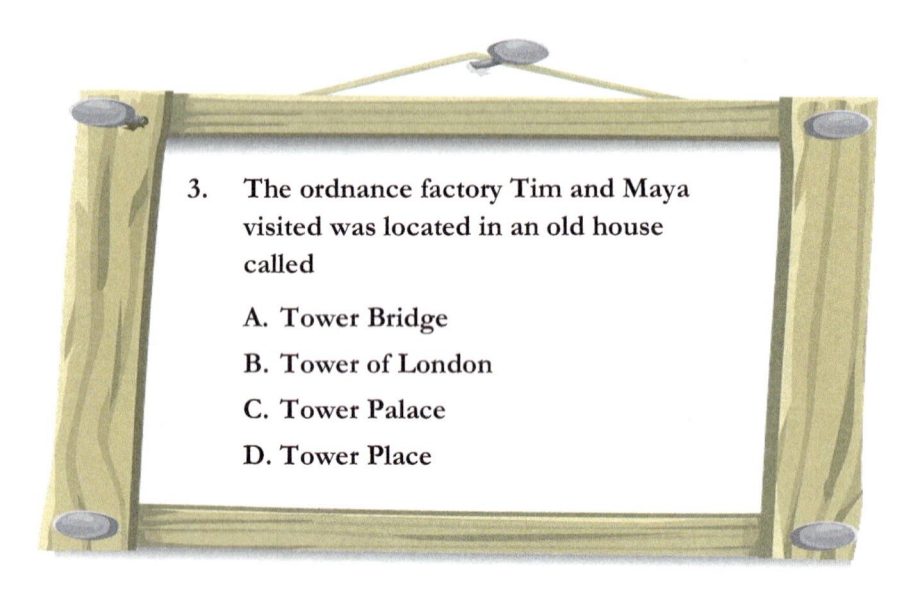

   A. Medway
   B. Fleet
   C. Thames
   D. Tyburn

3. The ordnance factory Tim and Maya visited was located in an old house called

   A. Tower Bridge
   B. Tower of London
   C. Tower Palace
   D. Tower Place

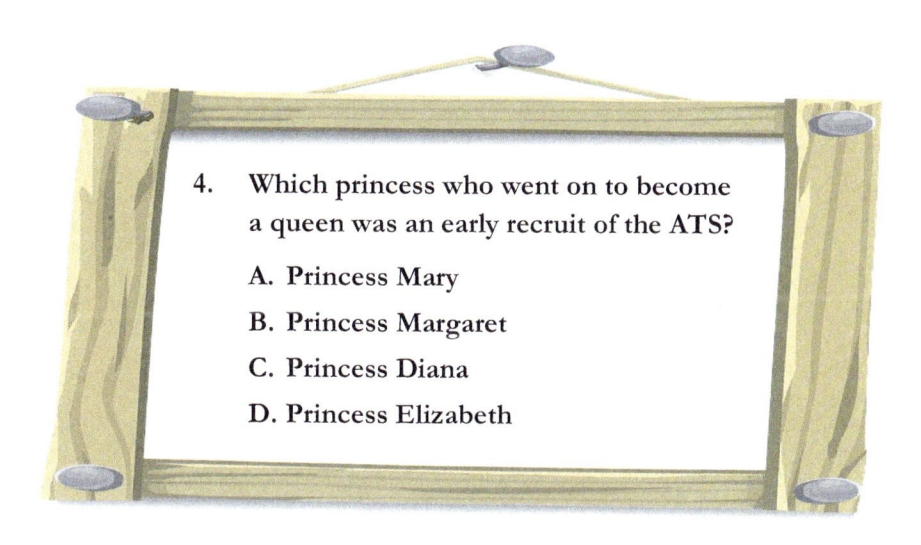

4. Which princess who went on to become a queen was an early recruit of the ATS?

   A. Princess Mary
   B. Princess Margaret
   C. Princess Diana
   D. Princess Elizabeth

5. Which one of the following was a work never given to women in the British military during WWII?

   A. nursing
   B. making weapons
   C. driving
   D. active combat

Chapter 7:

Pearl Harbor and America Enters the War

A Sneak Attack

That night, when everyone was sleeping in the Anderson Shelter outside the Hampton home, Tim and Maya closed their eyes, held onto the letters they had found in their pockets, and whispered, "Pearl Harbor, 1941." Sadly, they could not say goodbye to Thomas without telling him where they were headed.

After the familiar sensation of being pulled through a dark hole again, they landed on their feet in what looked like a street. Though it was night, all the lights in the streets and buildings were turned off. For a minute, Tim and Maya were terrified that the clock had taken them to the wrong place, but soon, it became clear that they were in Pearl Harbor, very close to the U.S. Naval base.

Tim and Maya quickly climbed through an open, dark window into a building and hid behind the door of some wall cabinets. Soon, some naval men filed into the room, closed all the windows, drew the blinds, and only then switched on the lights. Tim and Maya could see this was a meeting and waited to hear what they would discuss.

One senior and distinguished-looking American naval officer said, "President Roosevelt declared war on Japan yesterday. We have no time to lose. In the Japanese attack masterminded by Admiral Isoroku Yamamoto, we lost three of our battleships. Using warships carrying fighter planes, the Japanese used both their navy and air force to attack our ships at rest. USS *Arizona*, USS *Oklahoma*, and USS *Utah* are lost and are beyond mending. The rest of them, though damaged, can be repaired and put on sea again. We will be issued new orders to move toward Japanese targets, but for now, we recoup and wait. Meanwhile, to protect ourselves from further Japanese air raids, this entire base must ensure blackouts at night. Rationing of food and fuel will start soon as well."

From the rest of the speech, Tim and Maya gathered that though America had been hit badly, since all the American battleships were docked in the shallow waters of Battleship Row in Pearl Harbor, except for the three that were heavily damaged, the rest had not sunk to the bottom of the ocean. This might prove costly to the Japanese soon.

His words were met with many questions from the other sailors, all of which the senior officer answered calmly. Tim and Maya understood that the attack on Pearl Harbor had surprised the American Navy. They hadn't had the time to respond. More than once the men spoke of the Japanese "sneak attack," which had been planned in advance by Japan's Imperial Navy to try and destroy American warships and weaken their defenses.

Day of Infamy

The two children could sense the men were extremely angry. The USA, from the beginning of the war, had maintained its position of not directly attacking the Axis Powers, though they were sending supplies to support Great Britain. The American policy had been to build up its defenses without angering either Allied or Axis countries. America was just out of the economic depression after the Great War, and they did not want to get involved in this "foreign, European" War.

After this attack, however, America couldn't just sit back doing nothing. After President Franklin D. Roosevelt's speech a day ago, in which he had called the day of the Pearl Harbor attack—December 7, 1941—"a day of infamy," (FDR's "Day of Infamy" speech, 2001) the entire Congress, except for a single pacifist vote, voted in favor of war. Even American civilians, who had so far only hoped to avoid another war, were now screaming for revenge.

Tim thought war had a strange way of changing people's opinions when their own country, family, and loved ones were under threat.

When the meeting was over and the men left, Tim and Maya came out of their hiding place and quickly left the building. They wanted to look around at what was happening in the surrounding areas. Though the Japanese attack had mainly aimed to destroy the U.S. Naval base in Pearl Harbor, many civilians too had lost lives and property in the two-hour attack that happened early in the morning on December 7.

As daylight came, they saw people being evacuated and moving away with whatever little possessions they had been able to save. Tim and Maya could see people working hard to rescue others, providing help and shelter to the injured and homeless. From people talking to each other and news reports, the children learned that around 2,400 people, including soldiers, marines, sailors, and civilians, were killed. It was not just Americans but also native Hawaiians on the island of Oahu who had been injured and killed. The children saw that the local people and the Navy wanted nothing more than to rebuild the place and their lives.

From their conversation with John at the museum, Tim and Maya knew that there was one big battle that was a direct result of the Pearl Harbor attack. They used the clock to take themselves six months ahead to the Pacific Theater of the war.

Do You Know?

- **Pearl Harbor's radar detection:** On the morning of December 7, 1941, a U.S. Army radar station in Hawaii picked up signals of incoming aircraft. The radar operators noticed a large group of planes, but when they reported it, their warning was dismissed. Officers assumed the blips on the radar were U.S. B-17 bombers expected to arrive that day from the mainland. Because of this, no immediate action was taken, allowing the Japanese planes to launch their surprise attack without interference.

- **Submarines in the attack:** While the Japanese air strike at Pearl Harbor was devastating, it wasn't the only method used. The Japanese also sent five small submarines known as "midget subs" to sneak into the harbor and assist in the attack. These submarines were only about 80 feet long and carried two crew members each. Only one of the midget subs made it into Pearl Harbor, and it managed to fire its torpedoes, but with little success. Afterward, four of the five submarines were sunk or captured, showing just how difficult their mission was.

Key Words

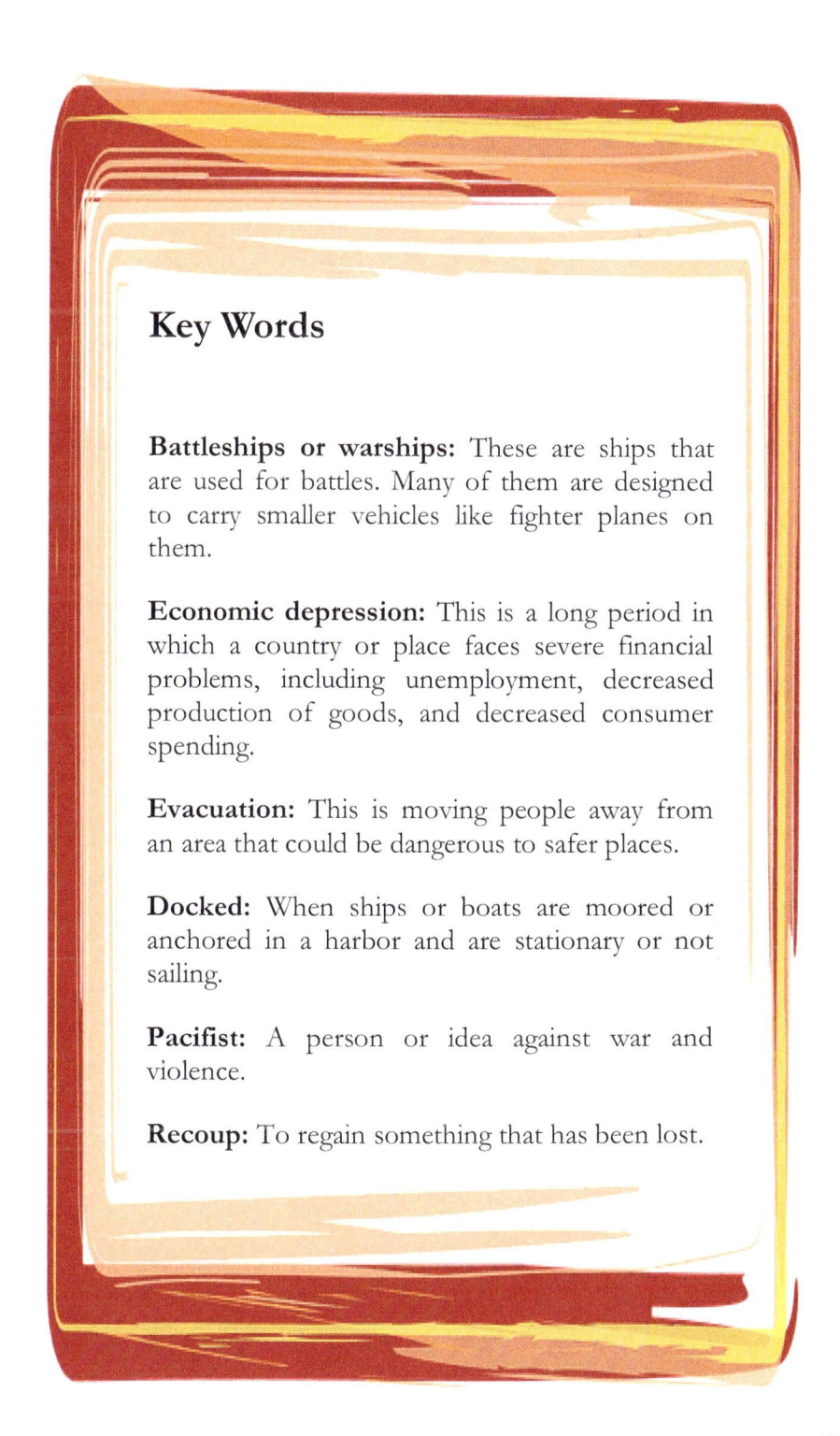

Battleships or warships: These are ships that are used for battles. Many of them are designed to carry smaller vehicles like fighter planes on them.

Economic depression: This is a long period in which a country or place faces severe financial problems, including unemployment, decreased production of goods, and decreased consumer spending.

Evacuation: This is moving people away from an area that could be dangerous to safer places.

Docked: When ships or boats are moored or anchored in a harbor and are stationary or not sailing.

Pacifist: A person or idea against war and violence.

Recoup: To regain something that has been lost.

Quiz

1. When did America declare war on Japan?

    A. December 7, 1941

    B. December 8, 1941

    C. December 9, 1941

    D. December 10, 1941

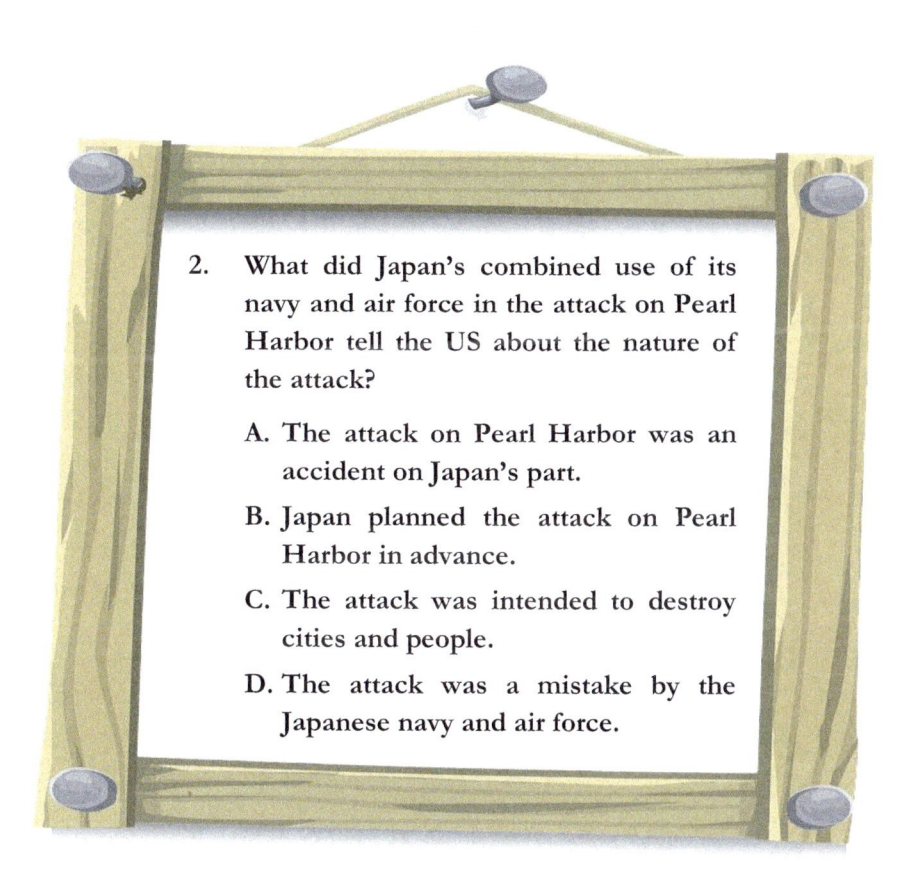

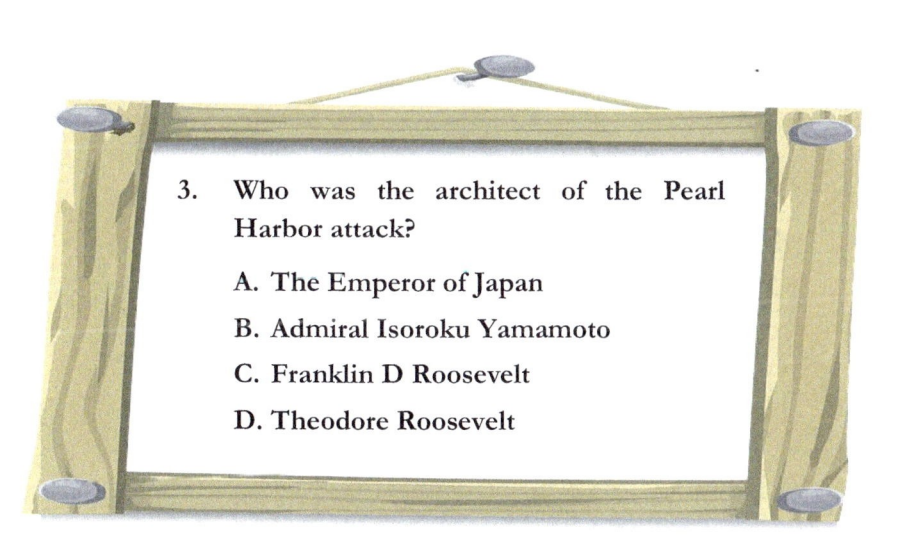

2. What did Japan's combined use of its navy and air force in the attack on Pearl Harbor tell the US about the nature of the attack?

   A. The attack on Pearl Harbor was an accident on Japan's part.
   B. Japan planned the attack on Pearl Harbor in advance.
   C. The attack was intended to destroy cities and people.
   D. The attack was a mistake by the Japanese navy and air force.

3. Who was the architect of the Pearl Harbor attack?

   A. The Emperor of Japan
   B. Admiral Isoroku Yamamoto
   C. Franklin D Roosevelt
   D. Theodore Roosevelt

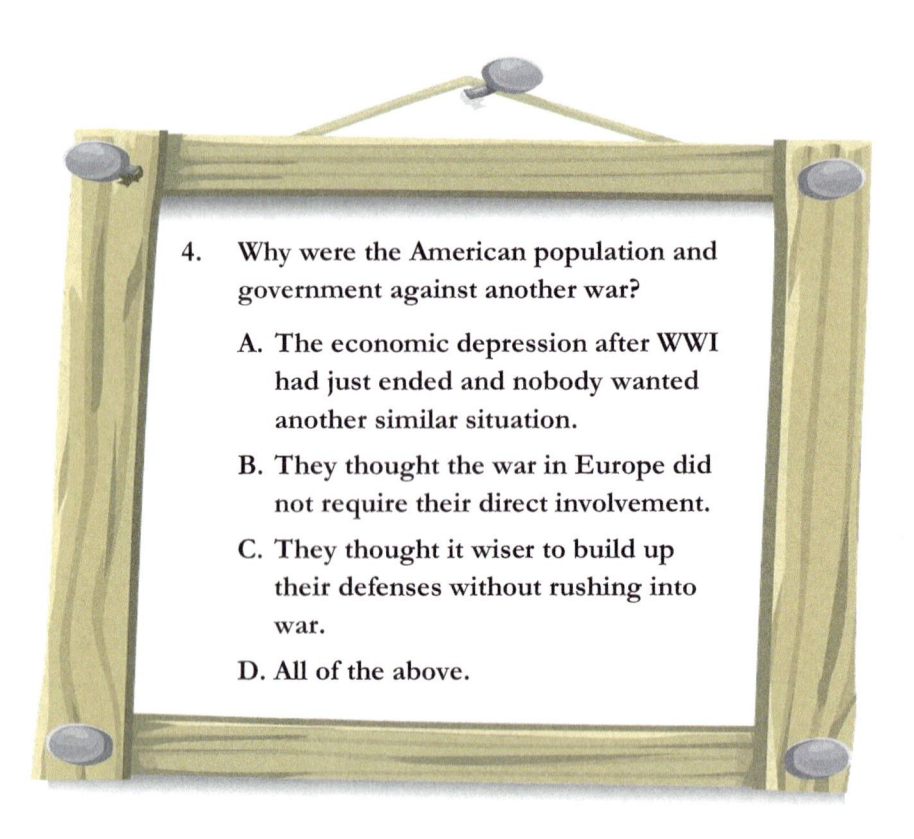

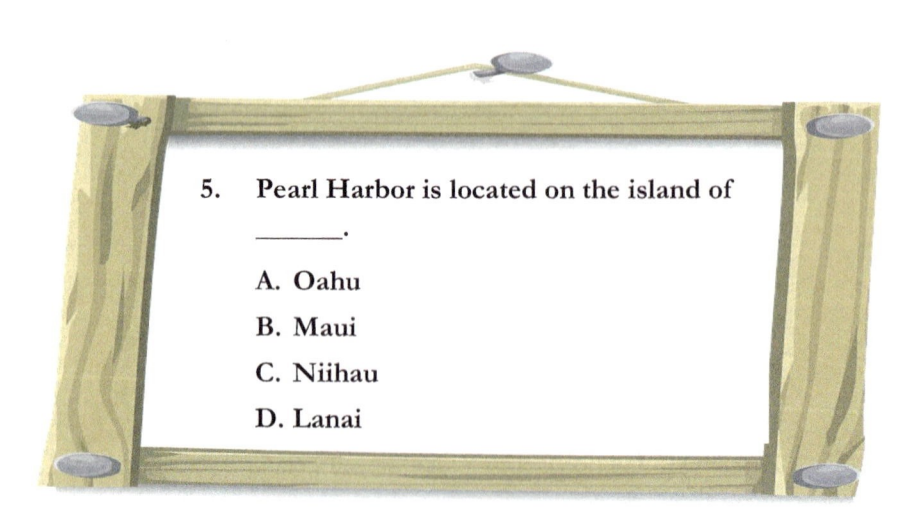

4. Why were the American population and government against another war?

   A. The economic depression after WWI had just ended and nobody wanted another similar situation.

   B. They thought the war in Europe did not require their direct involvement.

   C. They thought it wiser to build up their defenses without rushing into war.

   D. All of the above.

5. Pearl Harbor is located on the island of _____.

   A. Oahu
   B. Maui
   C. Niihau
   D. Lanai

Chapter 8:

The Battle of Midway

Operation MI

Tim and Maya used the clock's magic again. This time, when they opened their eyes, they knew they were in the thick of things. The swaying motion of the floor beneath them told them they were on a vessel floating on water. From the strong smell of salt, they knew they were out on the seas. They were hidden in cabinets on a warship!

If this wasn't scary enough, Maya asked whether they might be on the enemy ship! They definitely did not want to be caught by the Japanese or the Germans. Just then, they heard two officers talking in English with the typical Southern American drawl and felt relieved.

The first man said to the other, "It's a good thing the cryptanalysts found out in time the Japs had plans to attack Midway Atoll. We really have the codebreakers to thank for our knowledge of Operation MI."

The second sailor said, "The battle's just started. We know the Japanese attack on the Aleutian Islands is just a diversion and that their real target is Midway. It's a pity our fighter planes couldn't do more harm to their force."

The first man said, "At least their early morning aerial bombing still left Midway operational. Our fleet is already on its way to meet the Japanese. Hopefully, they will be unprepared enough to make mistakes."

Suddenly, a man came running in and was shouting something. Tim and Maya tensed, hoping it wasn't bad news.

Eventually, what he said made sense to them, "The *Akagi*, *Kaga*, and *Soryu* have been taken down by our bombers! They are three carriers down!"

The children understood three of the Japanese aircraft carriers had been destroyed and that this was indeed a turning point for the American Navy.

The Battle of Midway—Naval Warfare

The battle lasted only two days more. By the evening of that day, the U.S. Navy was having more success in shooting down Japanese boats. Tim and Maya learned that with this lead, the U.S. boats and ships were chasing the Japanese and continuing their attacks so they could not reach the island of Midway.

There was a clash between the Japanese aircraft carrier *Hiryu* and the USS *Yorktown*. One of the biggest advantages the U.S. forces had was their Dauntless airplanes that could dive bomb enemy ships and boats. The Devastator torpedo strikes of the US weren't as effective, though they held back the Japanese to some extent. Though the *Yorktown* was abandoned, bombers from it returned to attack *Hiryu*.

Eventually, the *Hiryu*, the last of the Japanese carriers, was set on fire, too. They only had smaller ships, boats, and aerial bombers, which had nowhere to land now that the carriers were all gone.

In two days, Tim and Maya learned that the Japanese forces were retreating because their casualties were too high for them to keep attacking the U.S. vessels. And so, the Battle OF Midway lasted only three days, from June 3-6, 1942.

Once ashore, Tim and Maya learned that the Japanese had lost more than 3,000 men, all four of their carriers, and 300 planes. These were the same carriers they had used in attacking the Americans at Pearl Harbor. The Americans lost 360 men, the carrier USS *Yorktown*, the destroyer *Hamman*, and 145 aircraft.

Tim and Maya knew the Pacific Theater of the war was now in the safe hands of the U.S. Navy. For the rest of the war, the Japanese wouldn't dream of attacking aggressively. They would instead focus only on defending themselves.

Next, a discussion between two navy men led Tim to hear the words "the Battle of El Alamein." Tim told Maya they would head there next and find out all about it.

Do You Know?

Well-known Hollywood director John Ford filmed the battle as part of his role as an officer in the U.S. Naval Reserve. He was assigned the job of creating documentaries for the Navy during World War II. While stationed on Midway during the battle, he was injured from a gunshot wound and became concussed from a Japanese attack. Despite this, he remained at his post until he got the footage. His recordings were included in the film *The Battle of Midway* (1942), for which he received the Oscar for Best Documentary.

Key Words

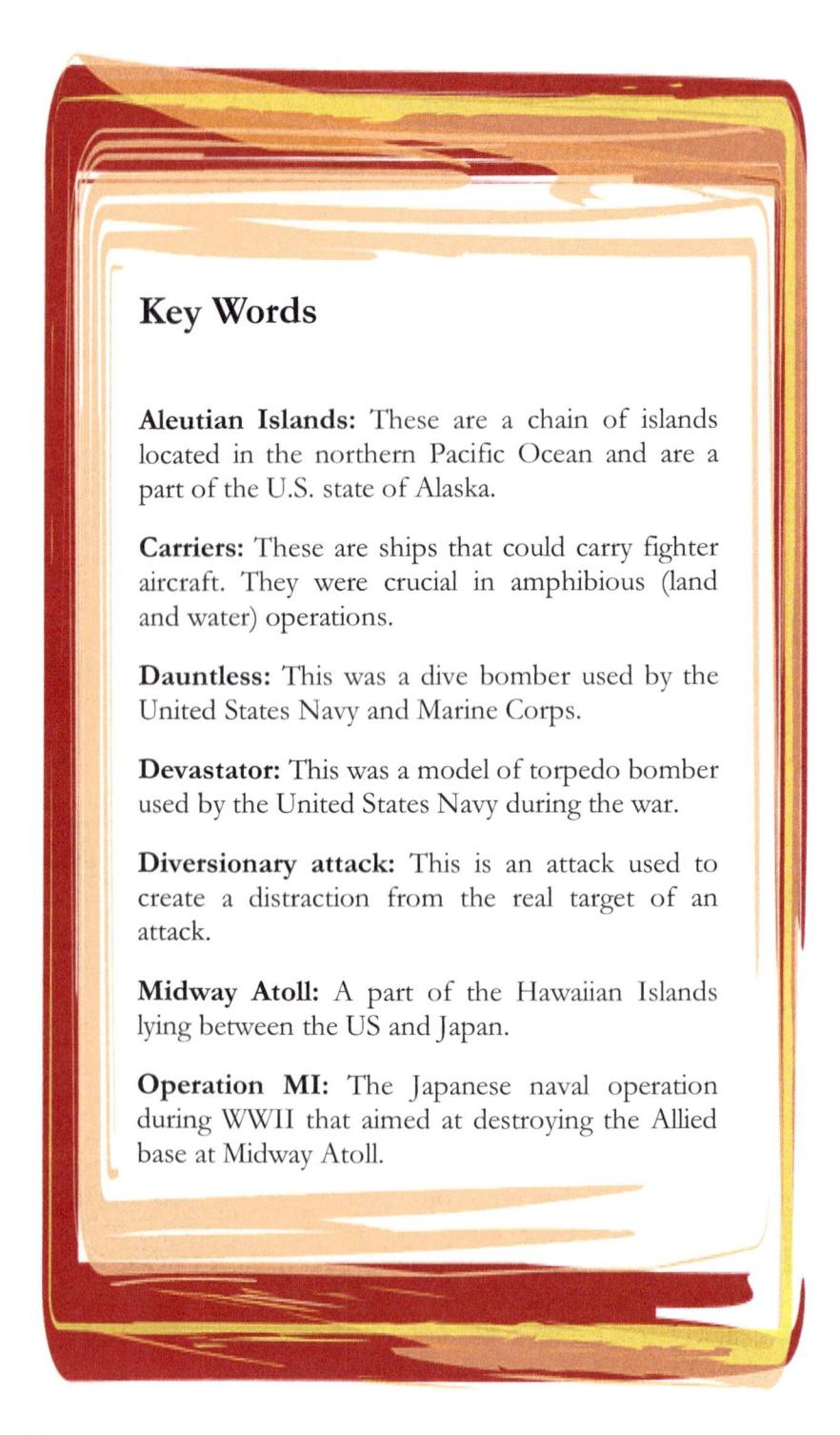

Aleutian Islands: These are a chain of islands located in the northern Pacific Ocean and are a part of the U.S. state of Alaska.

Carriers: These are ships that could carry fighter aircraft. They were crucial in amphibious (land and water) operations.

Dauntless: This was a dive bomber used by the United States Navy and Marine Corps.

Devastator: This was a model of torpedo bomber used by the United States Navy during the war.

Diversionary attack: This is an attack used to create a distraction from the real target of an attack.

Midway Atoll: A part of the Hawaiian Islands lying between the US and Japan.

Operation MI: The Japanese naval operation during WWII that aimed at destroying the Allied base at Midway Atoll.

Quiz

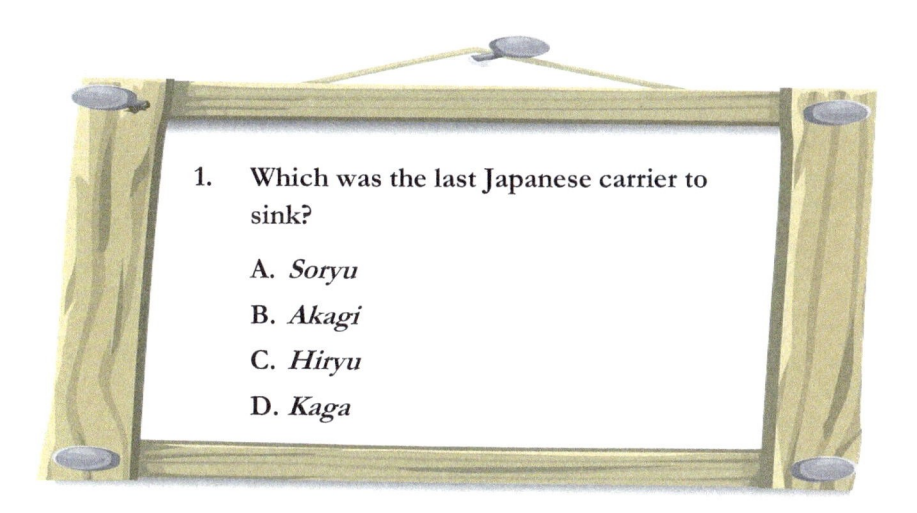

1. Which was the last Japanese carrier to sink?

    A. *Soryu*

    B. *Akagi*

    C. *Hiryu*

    D. *Kaga*

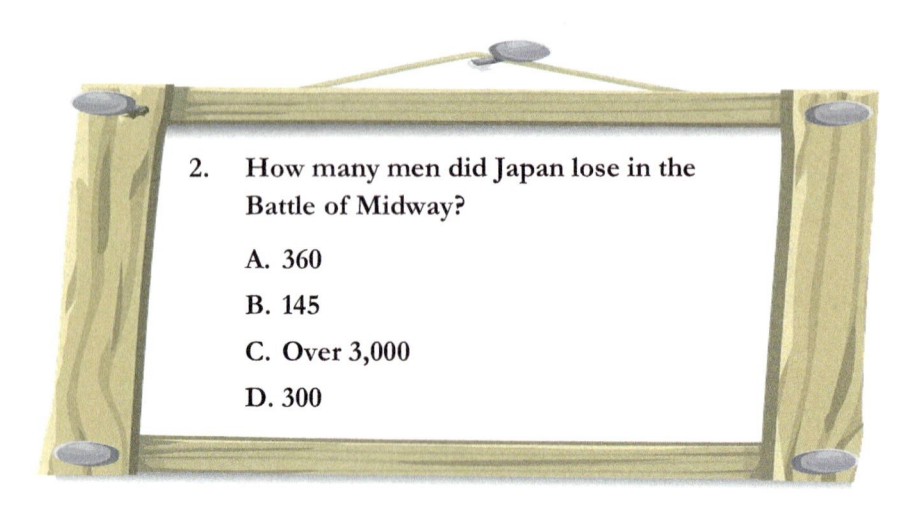

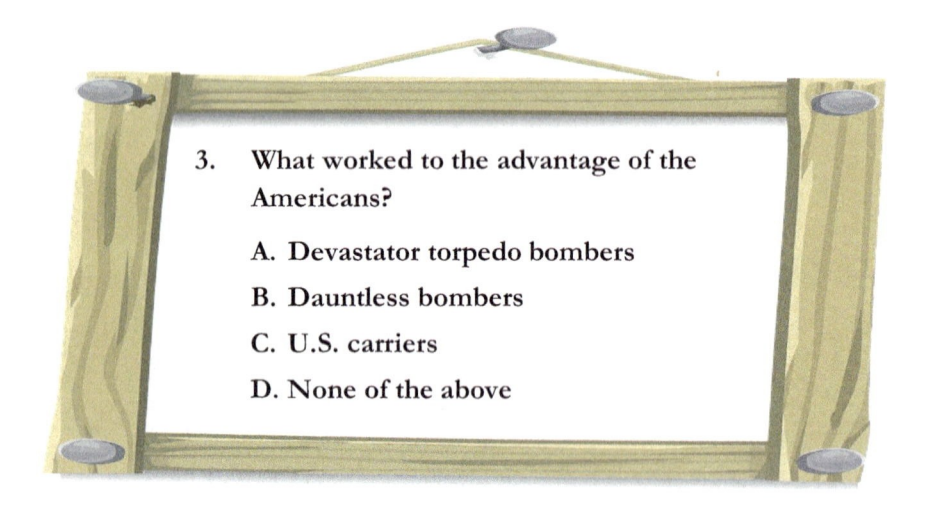

2. How many men did Japan lose in the Battle of Midway?

A. 360

B. 145

C. Over 3,000

D. 300

3. What worked to the advantage of the Americans?

A. Devastator torpedo bombers

B. Dauntless bombers

C. U.S. carriers

D. None of the above

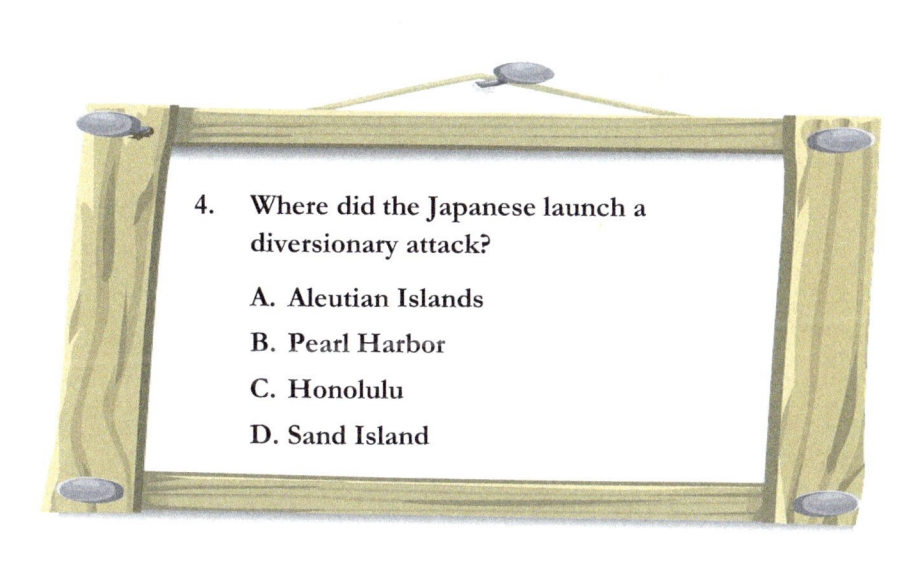

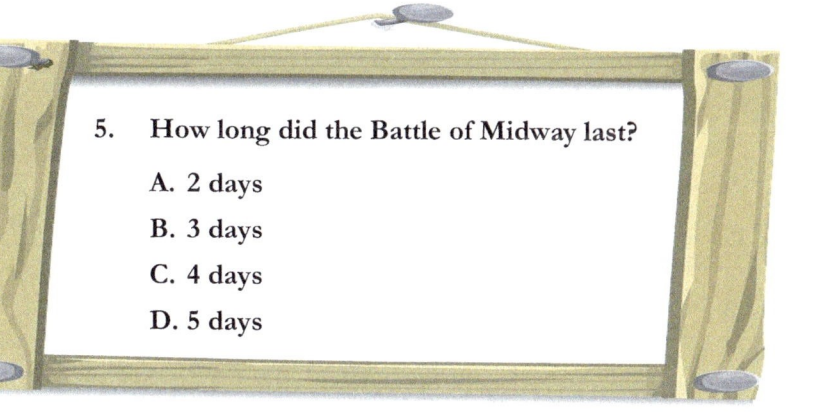

4. Where did the Japanese launch a diversionary attack?

   A. Aleutian Islands
   B. Pearl Harbor
   C. Honolulu
   D. Sand Island

5. How long did the Battle of Midway last?

   A. 2 days
   B. 3 days
   C. 4 days
   D. 5 days

Chapter 9:

The Battle of El Alamein

Tim and Maya were more interested in learning about the results of the Battle of El Alamein than watching it in real time. What they heard and saw in the Battle of Midway was enough to let them know that war wasn't their thing. They decided to travel six months ahead to El Alamein, Egypt. As before, they felt the pull of the clock as they were pushed through an invisible dark tunnel. Finally, they landed on solid ground. From their calculations, they guessed correctly that it was December 1942 in El Alamein.

Tim and Maya landed in broad daylight in what looked like a peaceful seaside town in Egypt. Asking questions of a few English-speaking people they came across, they understood that El Alamein was only about 72 miles away from the great city of Alexandria and about 170 miles from Cairo, the capital of Egypt. Suddenly, it dawned on Tim and Maya why winning at El Alamein was so important for the Allies and Axis Powers: Whoever won could control Egypt and the valuable oil reserves in the Middle Eastern regions. The victor would also be in charge of the Suez Canal between Africa and Europe, shortening travel time between the two continents.

They saw that the British forces were still present in El Alamein. This could only mean one thing—an Allied victory! They wanted to hear the full story from one of the soldiers who had fought the battle and was willing to tell them everything that happened in full detail.

The soldier, whose name was Jeremy, was off-duty for a while. The soldiers weren't given long leaves to go home, of course, but they could take a day or two for personal reasons as long as there was no active combat and they did not wander far from the army base. He had come into the city to sightsee a bit.

The Second Battle of El Alamein—Desert and Ground Warfare

Operation Lightfoot

Jeremy said, "El Alamein was two battles, actually. The first one was between July 1-27 this year, while the second one, in which we won, lasted from October 23–November 11. The Allies, made up of the British, South Africans, New Zealanders, Australians, Indians, and the French, fought against Germans and Italians. The US helped us by supplying their Sherman Tanks and other weaponry, though they did not actively participate in the combat."

Tim asked, "So, why were there two wars?"

Jeremy said, "Well, the First Battle of Alamein led nowhere. We call it a *stalemate* when neither army can make any progress. Our leader for the first war, General Claude Auchinleck, was able to stop the German–Italian progress into Egypt, but we couldn't beat them. Prime Minister Churchill replaced Auchinleck with General Bernard Montgomery, known for his tactical warfare. General Montgomery lost no time in making many changes in the structure of our army unit here. I can still hear his uplifting and encouraging speeches. He once said he would 'hit Rommel for six out of Africa'" (BBC, 2014).

Jeremey stopped to chuckle a bit. The children did not understand this reference to the game of cricket, a popular British sport in which a batsman, who could hit the bowler's ball outside the boundaries of the field without it touching the ground, earned his team six runs.

Jeremy continued, "We faced a strong enemy, especially because they were being led by the experienced General Erwin Romel. He is not called the 'Desert Fox' for nothing! He really knew how to use his weapons and men. But he left for Germany in mid-September. It was rumored that he was unwell. He left command of the Italian and German Panzerarmee to his subordinate. This was good for us."

Maya asked, "So, what did General Montgomery do?

Jeremy replied, "The General was smart. He planned the attack in two operations. The first one was called Operation Lightfoot, which started on October 23rd. Through continuous artillery bombardment and attacks by our infantry, we could cut through the German line though not crumble it. They were strong."

Tim asked, "What was the second phase?"

Operation Supercharge

Jeremy said, "That was Operation Supercharge which we launched on November 1st. The infantry divisions cleared the path so the armored divisions could sweep in. Interestingly, we used a lot of trick tactics. Many of our real tanks were disguised as trucks, and we used inflated dummy tanks to trick the Germans into believing we were stronger than them. The German army got tired and overwhelmed. Though General Rommel had returned to lead them, even he felt that retreat was the only option. We heard Hitler wanted him to 'stand and fight' to the last man but Rommel removed his forces by the 4th of November."

Maya asked, "So, have all the Axis forces left?"

Jeremy said, "We still continue to chase them out, but they are too few and far apart to pose any real threat to our base here in Africa. We also strengthened our hold on Africa through Operation Torch on November 8th."

Tim asked, "What's that?"

Jeremey answered, "Americans and the British landed in French-occupied Northern African colonies such as Morocco and Algiers. Earlier, the Vichy Government of France, under the Germans, controlled the armies here. However, by November 10th, the French military authorities signed an armistice with the Allies. They did not really want to fight the stronger Allies. Most of them eventually joined and are fighting alongside us too. Unfortunately, this has led to Germany overrunning the whole of France. They had Northern France in control since 1940, but after Operation Torch, they have occupied the whole of France."

Tim and Maya talked for a while more with their new friend until Jeremy had to report back to his commanding officer. The children had heard so much about France under German rule that they wanted to know how its liberation took place. They decided to go to Paris next.

Do You Know?

- The Battle of El Alamein was one of the biggest turning points for the Allies. Winston Churchill called it the "end of the beginning." He also said that this particular battle was important because until then the Allies had no major victories, but after it, they had no defeats.

- The Allied soldiers who fought in El Alamein were called the "Rats of Tobruk"—a mocking name a Nazi radio broadcaster gave them. However, the brave Allied soldiers gave the Axis troops a lot of trouble, especially in many guerilla attacks in the underground passages and caves of Tobruk, a place on the Libyan–Egyptian border. They were proud to be the "rats" against Rommel's "Desert Fox."

- Erwin Rommel was respected even among the Allies because he promoted "war without hatred." He was known to be an experienced, brave soldier and commander who did not support the Nazi ideology. He was suspected of the anti-Nazi plot to assassinate Hitler in 1944. Since the Nazi government could not execute him without angering the German people, who considered him a national hero, they gave him three choices: to defend himself, face the people's court, or commit suicide. He chose the last in exchange for the safety of his family and a reputable death. In Germany, he was given a state funeral with full military honors for his services in WWI and WWII.

Key Words

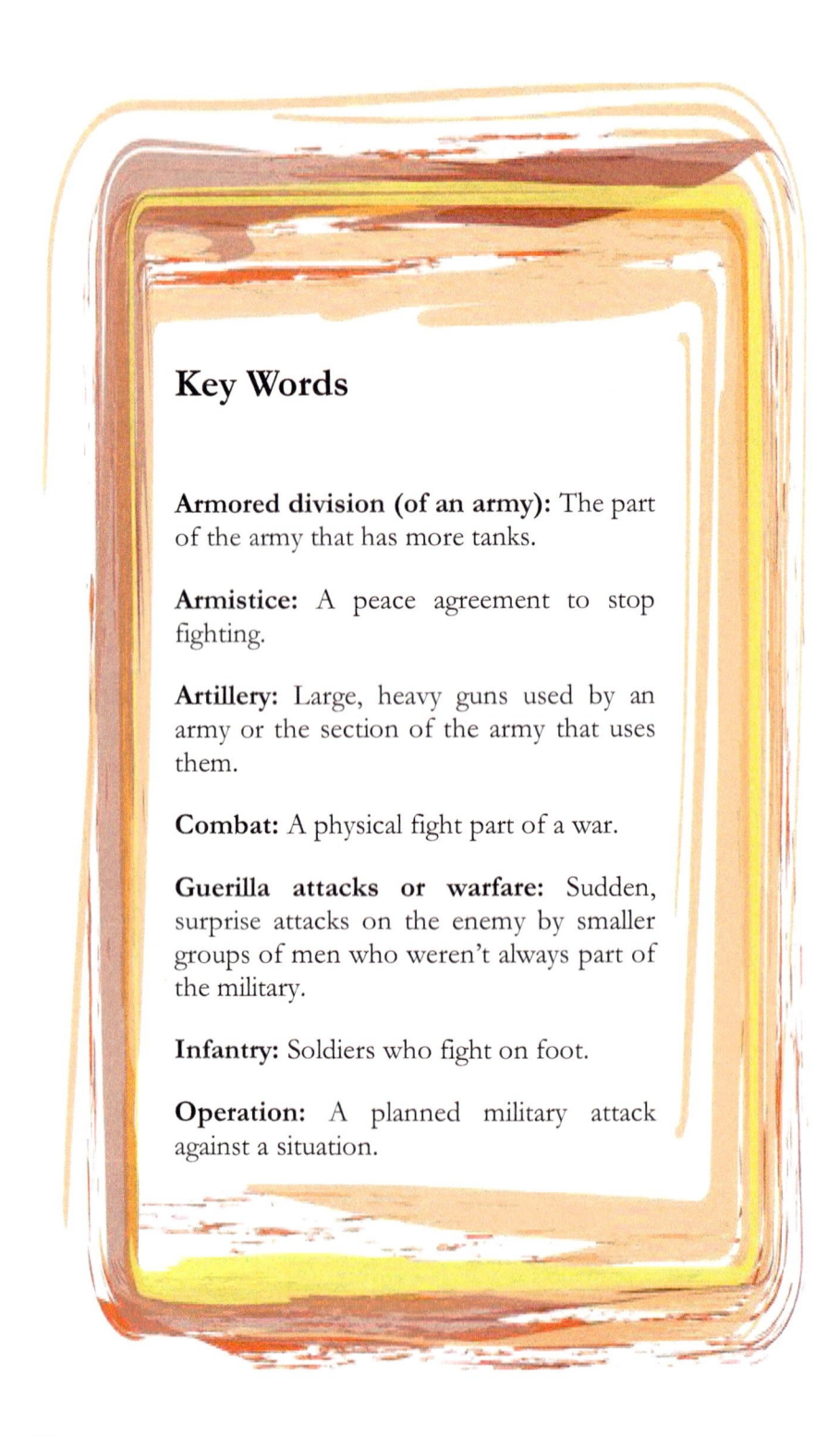

Armored division (of an army): The part of the army that has more tanks.

Armistice: A peace agreement to stop fighting.

Artillery: Large, heavy guns used by an army or the section of the army that uses them.

Combat: A physical fight part of a war.

Guerilla attacks or warfare: Sudden, surprise attacks on the enemy by smaller groups of men who weren't always part of the military.

Infantry: Soldiers who fight on foot.

Operation: A planned military attack against a situation.

Panzerarmee: The armored tank divisions of the German and Italian forces.

Stalemate: In a battle refers to a situation where neither side is able to secure a victory or make significant advancements.

Quiz

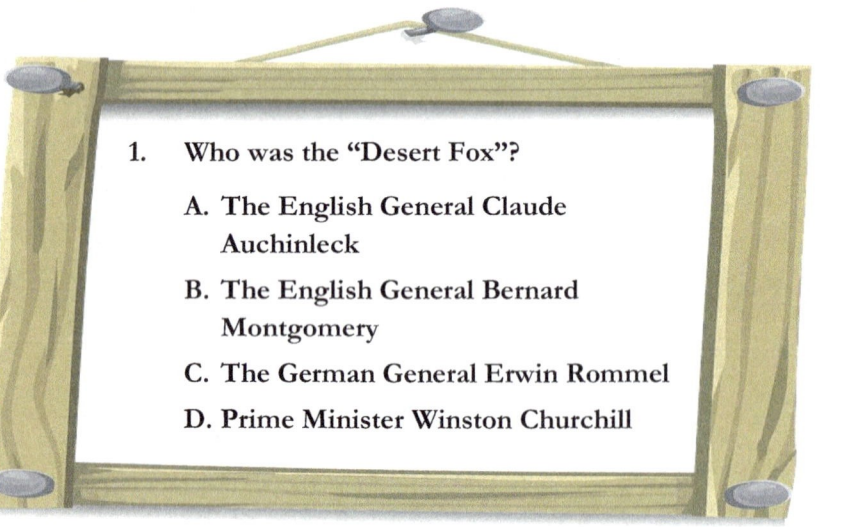

1. Who was the "Desert Fox"?

   A. The English General Claude Auchinleck

   B. The English General Bernard Montgomery

   C. The German General Erwin Rommel

   D. Prime Minister Winston Churchill

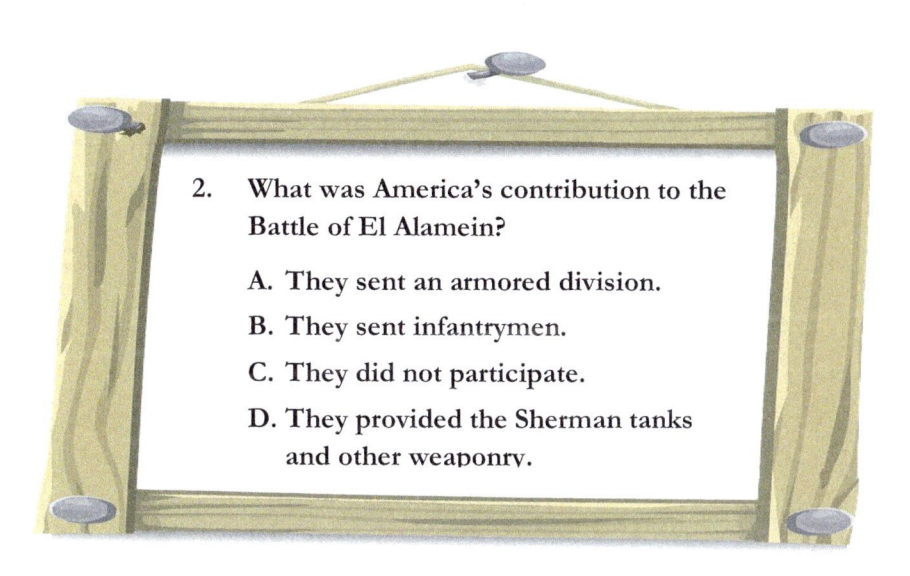

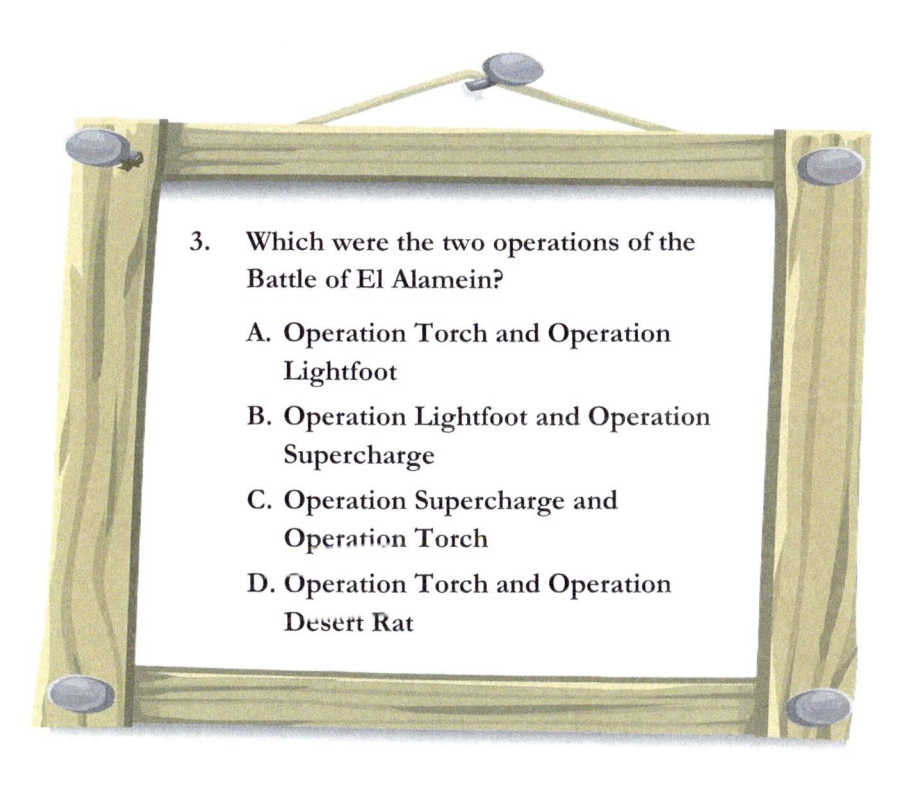

2. What was America's contribution to the Battle of El Alamein?

   A. They sent an armored division.
   B. They sent infantrymen.
   C. They did not participate.
   D. They provided the Sherman tanks and other weaponry.

3. Which were the two operations of the Battle of El Alamein?

   A. Operation Torch and Operation Lightfoot
   B. Operation Lightfoot and Operation Supercharge
   C. Operation Supercharge and Operation Torch
   D. Operation Torch and Operation Desert Rat

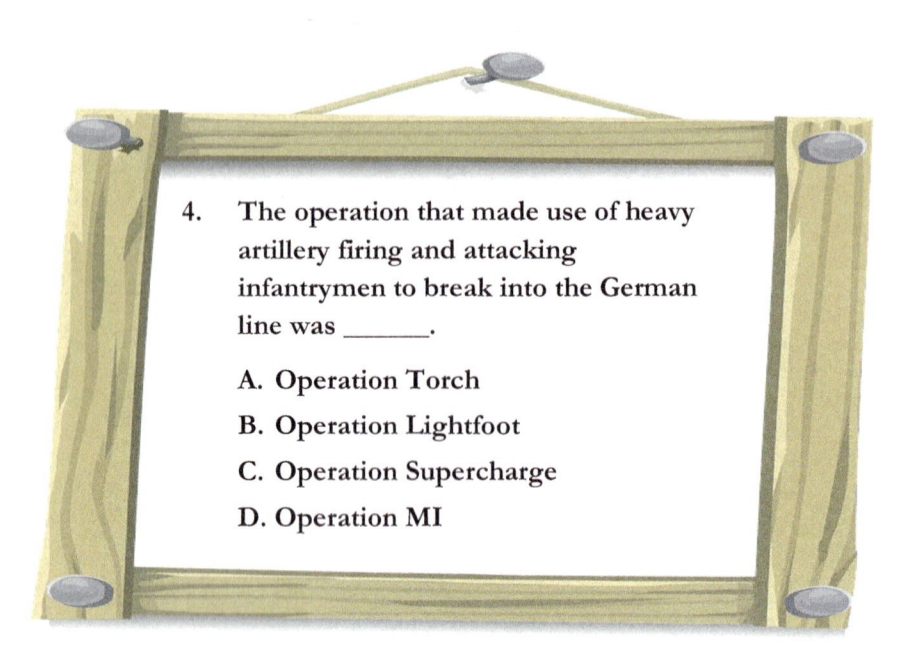

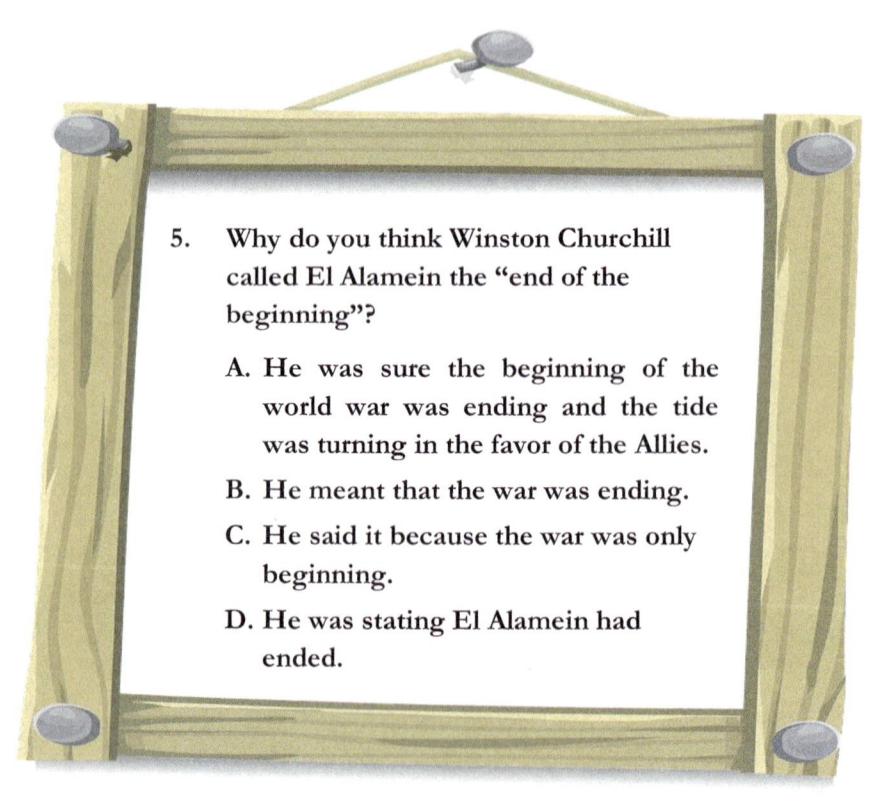

4. The operation that made use of heavy artillery firing and attacking infantrymen to break into the German line was _____.

   A. Operation Torch
   B. Operation Lightfoot
   C. Operation Supercharge
   D. Operation MI

5. Why do you think Winston Churchill called El Alamein the "end of the beginning"?

   A. He was sure the beginning of the world war was ending and the tide was turning in the favor of the Allies.
   B. He meant that the war was ending.
   C. He said it because the war was only beginning.
   D. He was stating El Alamein had ended.

Chapter 10:

D-Day and the Liberation of France

The Battle of Normandy

Tim and Maya knew they had to act quickly before the clock's magic ran out. They knew Paris was liberated on August 25, 1944—a date John, their guide at the museum, had mentioned. They said aloud the date and place and wished hard. When they opened their eyes, they were on the streets where people had gathered, waving white handkerchiefs and shouting out happily.

Tim and Maya stood next to a lady, holding up an English placard (unlike most of the others who had them in French) reading "Freedom to Paris! Freedom to France!"

Maya asked her innocently, "Hi, I'm Maya, could you explain what's happening?"

The lady said, "Hi Maya, I'm Dolores. The Allied troops are coming in any time now. We all heard it broadcast on the radio. After more than four years of Nazi rule, France is finally going to be free!"

Maya asked her, "How did that happen?"

Dolores smiled and said, "Oh, dear! Where do I start? More than two months ago, the Allied troops launched air-water-land attacks on the North coast of France. They landed their troops in Normandy on June 6th, in an operation aptly named "Overlord." This is why June 6th was called "D-Day" or "The Day." We hear that British, American, Canadian, and Free French forces landed on five beaches in Normandy. After Dunkirk in 1940, from where the British forces were forced to withdraw, this was the first time the Allies were gaining a foothold in Europe."

Tim spoke, "So, this was the beginning of the Battle of Normandy that we keep hearing about? Who led it?"

Dolores said, "Correct. Since Operation Overlord was mainly coordinated by the USA, General Dwight D. Eisenhower was the supreme commander of the Allied troops. Many British and American generals helped him form his plans. Mind you, he already had a lot of experience. He was the mastermind behind Operation Torch in Northern Africa and the invasions of Sicily and Rome in Italy."

Maya, who remembered her history lesson, was almost tempted to cry, "But that was our 34th president," when she remembered that moment was only yet to come. She asked instead, "Who led the defense?"

Dolores said, "Erwin Rommel played a big part. However, he reported to Commander in Chief West Gerd von Rundstedt. However, since France was a precious win for Germany, many of the decisions were taken directly by Adolf Hitler himself. Anyway, the Allies landed and slowly built up their defense with more troops landing via sea and air. Even before the landing, the Allies had been mounting airstrikes on all important French targets, cutting off the supply and transportation lines of the Germans. There wasn't much the Germans could do to prevent these landings."

Tim marveled, "That's so clever!"

Dolores laughed, "But that's not all. The Allies sent fake radio signals and used deception tactics to make the Germans believe the D-Day landings would be on the Seine at Pas de Calais, opposite Dover. They even created news about a phantom army of Allied forces in South East England preparing to attack—an army that did not exist. The poor Germans were kept guessing about the actual place of the landings until the day it happened. Even after the landings, dummies were parachuted instead of men, and inflatable tanks were used to confuse the Germans."

Maya asked, "Amazing! What happened then?"

Viva la Paris

Dolores said, "Well nothing is ever easy in war. Though the landings were successful, the Allies found it hard to proceed, with the Germans defending their territories ferociously. It took a while before the Americans and British could break into the German line of defense. But by July 25th, the Germans were getting frustrated. In Operation Cobra, the Allied Forces swept into Brittany. Well, it was the beginning. Though Hitler thought he could fight against the Allies, he soon saw how pointless it was. On August 16, he commanded the retreat of the German force, who started leaving quickly When the Resistance saw the Germans leaving, they increased their attacks, especially here in Paris."

Maya asked, "What is the Resistance?"

Dolores said, "They are the French people who are against the Nazi rule of France. They had been working underground and sending secret messages these last four years about German movements to the Allies. Of course, most of the Resistance were just ordinary people, so they did not have superior weapons. But they did what they could and all of the last few weeks, we've had many fights against the German garrisons left behind here. And now we are going to see the result."

She stopped as everyone started cheering more loudly than before.

The children could see military men marching into the Champs-Élysées, the street they were now at. The parade was led by a tall, thin man, as the soldiers walked to the Notre Dame Cathedral. They learned he was General Charles de Gaulle, the leader of the Free French Army that had been fighting against the Nazis alongside the Allies. People waved the French flag and shouted slogans of *"viva la Paris,"* which meant "long live Paris."

Paris, the "City of Light" or the "City of Love," was liberated because the German general left in charge of defending it, Dietrich von Choltitz, had signed the armistice with the Allies on August 25, 1944.

Do You Know?

- During World War II, after the capture of France in June 1940, France was split into two areas. The French government officially signed an armistice treaty and worked with the Germans. In return, the French Government was allowed to peacefully govern Southern France (the Free Zone) under General Philippe Pétain, a World War I hero. They shifted their base to Vichy in southern France. The Germans took control of Northern France (the Occupied Zone), including Paris. de Gaulle, along with members of the Free French Army and the French Resistance, were labeled as traitors by the Vichy government. Ultimately, when the Free French Army liberated France, the officials of the Vichy government faced trial for treason. Charles de Gaulle became the president and served his terms from 1944–1946 and from 1959–1969.

- The five beaches where the Allies landed on D-Day were code-named Utah, Omaha, Juno, Gold, and Sword Beaches.

Key Words

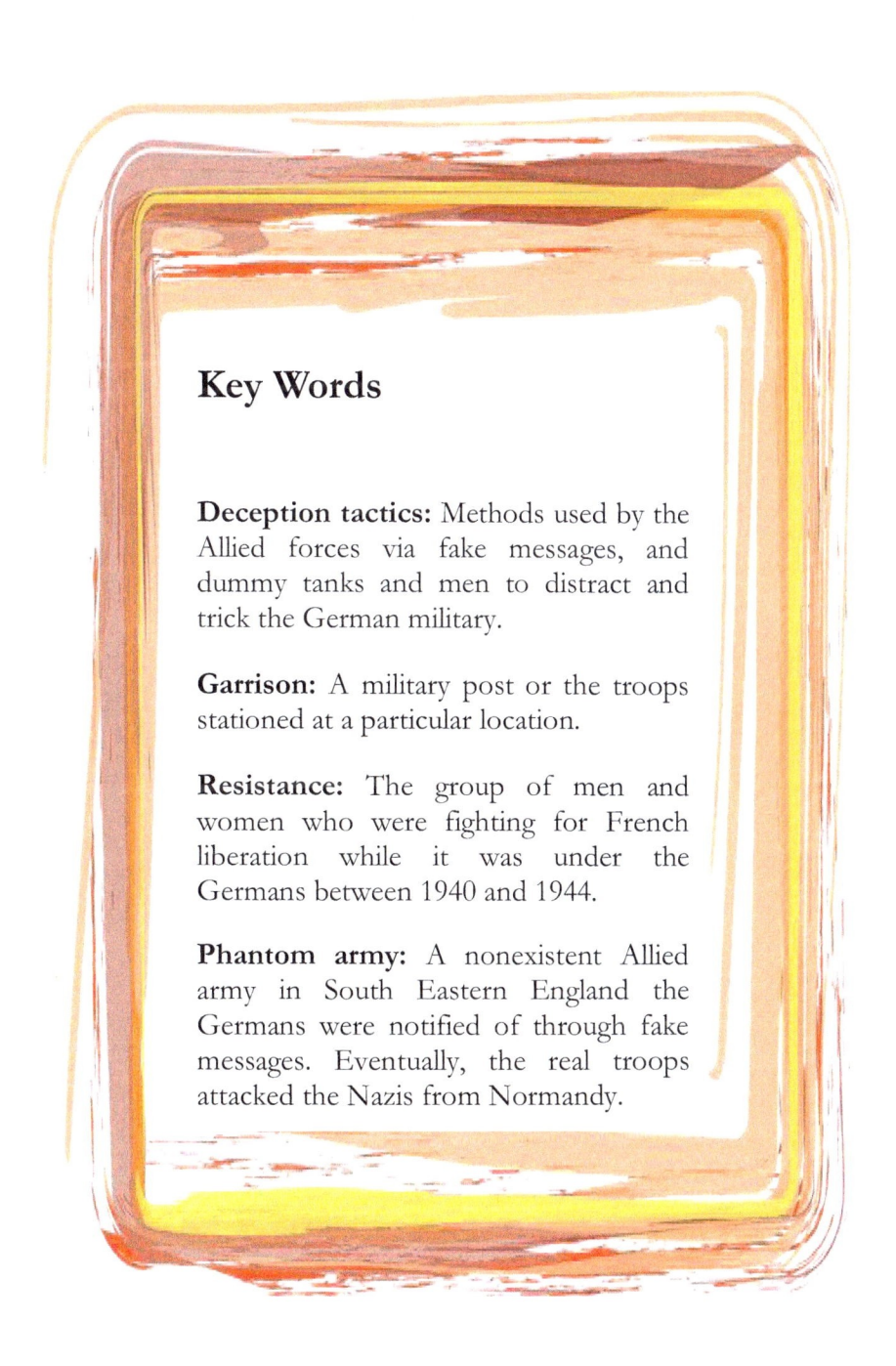

Deception tactics: Methods used by the Allied forces via fake messages, and dummy tanks and men to distract and trick the German military.

Garrison: A military post or the troops stationed at a particular location.

Resistance: The group of men and women who were fighting for French liberation while it was under the Germans between 1940 and 1944.

Phantom army: A nonexistent Allied army in South Eastern England the Germans were notified of through fake messages. Eventually, the real troops attacked the Nazis from Normandy.

Quiz

1. Who was the Free French Army Commander?

    A. Dwight Eisenhower

    B. Dietrich von Choltitz

    C. Charles de Gaulle

    D. Erwin Rommel

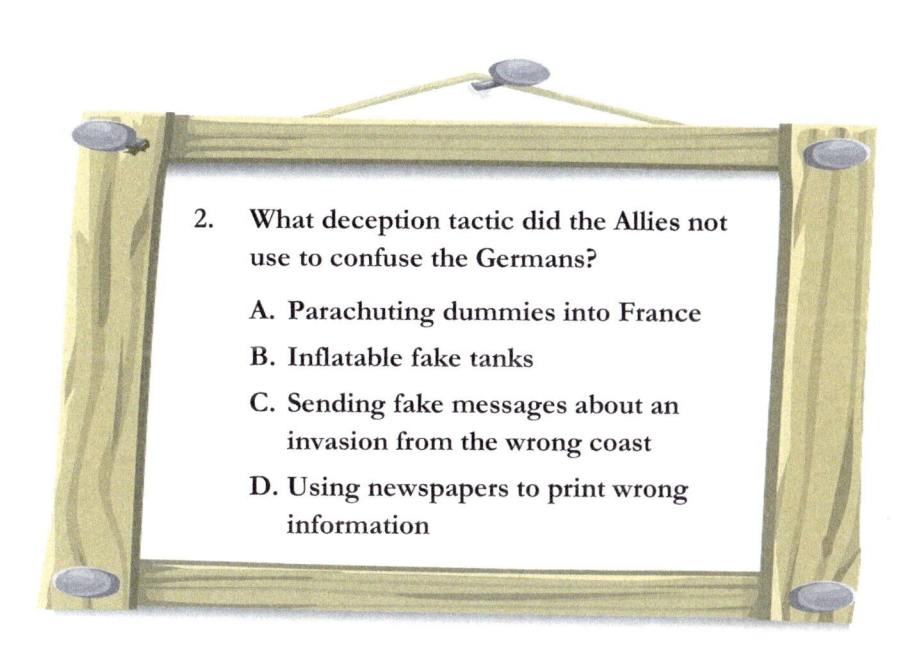

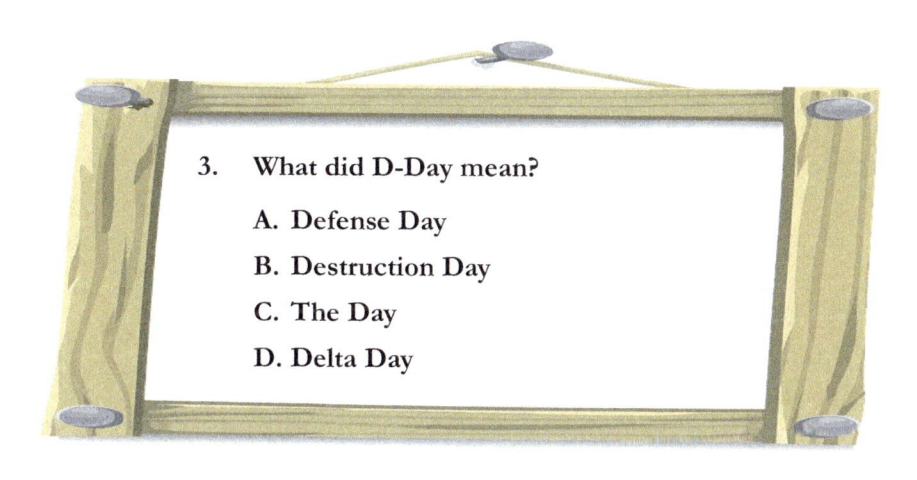

2. What deception tactic did the Allies not use to confuse the Germans?

   A. Parachuting dummies into France
   B. Inflatable fake tanks
   C. Sending fake messages about an invasion from the wrong coast
   D. Using newspapers to print wrong information

3. What did D-Day mean?

   A. Defense Day
   B. Destruction Day
   C. The Day
   D. Delta Day

4. Which American general who fought as the Supreme Commander of the Allied Forces went on to become a president?

   A. Franklin Roosevelt
   B. Dwight Eisenhower
   C. Philippe Pétain
   D. Charles de Gaulle

5. Paris is also called _____.

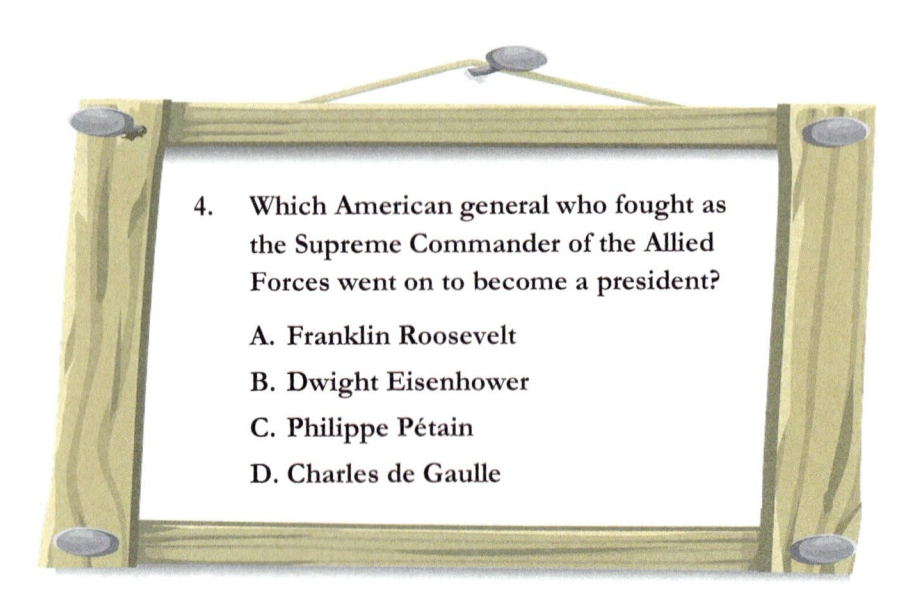

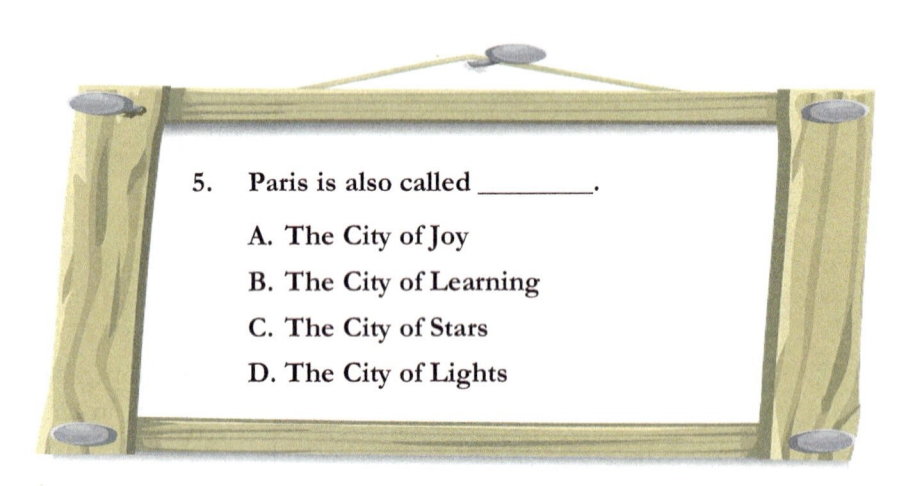

   A. The City of Joy
   B. The City of Learning
   C. The City of Stars
   D. The City of Lights

Chapter 11:

The Holocaust

Buchenwald, April 11, 1945

As Tim's and Maya's hearts swelled with pride at everything happening before their eyes in Paris, they heard two men behind them in the crowd discussing the "Nazi camp" near Weimar. Tim and Maya listened eagerly to understand what was being discussed. From schoolwork, they vaguely knew of the Jewish extermination camps across Europe. Tim and Maya did not realize these camps were the worst part of World War II. They decided to travel ahead in time to hear about the liberation of these camps.

Using the clock, Tim and Maya reached Weimar, a city in central Germany, about 186 miles from Berlin, where Adolf Hitler often met for meetings with his party. They chose mid-April 1945, a date which was only a month away from the Nazi surrender. By this time Allied troops would have already started invading Germany.

In the city, Tim and Maya met American soldiers who were talking about the horrors they saw at Buchenwald on April 11, 1945. Tim and Maya decided to talk further with them.

A young soldier named Harry agreed to tell them "a little" about the Buchenwald camp, which was very close to Weimar.

Tim asked him, "Why a little?"

Harry said, "Well, I'm not sure children should know too much about it. It was horrible. When we marched into Buchenwald a couple of days ago, we only thought it would be an ordinary prison where anti-Nazi people were held. We had also heard stories of it being an SS training camp."

Maya asked, "SS is the German police, right?"

Harry said, "Yes, it's short for *Schutzstaffel*, the special police of the Nazi government."

When Maya asked him to continue, he said, "When we entered, we saw that the camp had already been evacuated by the Germans. Maybe they did not want us to see what they had done. But we saw the dead bodies. They had used these camps not just to imprison people, but also to torture them and use them as slaves for construction and other war-building tasks. The survivors left behind were half-starved and looked like—there's no other word to describe them—walking skeletons. I did not see this, but I was told Nazi doctors and scientists conducted medical experiments on the prisoners, which killed them or made them very sick."

Tim and Maya gasped. They could not imagine such cruelty, especially from men of science or doctors.

Harry said, "But that's not even the worst. We found proof at the camp that prisoners the Germans felt were most "useless," like old people who couldn't work in labor camps, were sent off to other camps where they were put into gas chambers."

Maya asked without understanding, "What chambers?"

The soldier said, "Rooms that could be sealed after the prisoners were made to enter. Then carbon monoxide was let in, to kill them at a go. The prisoners were tricked into believing they were being led in for a bath. But actually, they were being poisoned."

Tim could only say, "Oh my!"

Tim and Maya felt so sad and upset discussing these that the soldier decided to stop telling them about the prisoner camps. The children were glad that these inhuman acts were brought to light and that at least some prisoners escaped death.

Tim and Maya went around Weimar and saw the death and destruction that had taken place here, too.

In a few weeks, they heard the news that Adolf Hitler committed suicide and that Germany was about to surrender. Berlin is where they would find out more, they thought.

The Horrors of the Holocaust

Buchenwald was only one of the many camps the Nazis created. There were thousands of such concentration camps where Jews, Blacks, people from countries conquered by the Nazis, political opponents of Nazism, the mentally challenged, and even prisoners of war were held. Anyone who Hitler thought stood between Germany's "progress" and his power was put into these camps.

The discrimination against Jews and others started little by little when the Nazi Party came into power with Hitler becoming the Chancellor in 1933. The Nuremberg Laws were passed in 1935, which took away the citizenship rights of Jews in Germany and German-occupied lands. Jews couldn't work, marry White Germans, and had to give up all their property. Some of them were driven away to other countries in the early days of the Third Reich.

Jews were identified and forced to wear armbands or badges with the Star of David on a yellow background. They were gathered, separated, and made to stay in districts called Jewish ghettoes, where living conditions were horrible. Ghettoes were very crowded, had food and water shortages, and had no heating or proper sanitation facilities. The prisoners were made to work in factories that produced Nazi Germany's weapons and buildings.

The Gestapo transported Jews and other prisoners slowly to concentration camps in Germany and Nazi-occupied European countries like Poland by train. The first of these camps was established at Dachau in 1933. Buchenwald was set up in 1937. One of the worst camps was Auschwitz-Birkenau in Poland, which had gas chambers for mass murders.

When Allied Forces marched to the concentration camps to liberate them starting in April 1945, they never imagined the torture and horrible conditions in which people were kept. Many soldiers, for whom the loss of life wasn't new, cried when they saw the starved prisoners and the thousands of bodies left behind by the Nazis.

The word "holocaust" comes from Greek and means "a completely burnt sacrifice." It was generally used to refer to any mass calamity that happened. Over time, it has become the name for the mass killing of Jews and other minorities during the Nazi rule. The Nazis called the killing of the Jews "The Final Solution." Before the Holocaust, the worldwide population of Jews was 16.5 million in 1939. Even today, 80 years after WWII, the number is only 16 million!

Do You Know?

- Heinrich Himmler, the SS leader, was the brains behind planning the concentration and death camps for Jews and other prisoners of the Nazi state. He is called the "Architect of the Holocaust." Like Hitler, Himmler, after his capture, committed suicide in May 1945.

- The Soviets liberated Majdanek in Lublin, Poland in July 1944. It was the first Nazi concentration camp to be set free. Photographs and videos of the insides of the camp proved the crimes of Nazi Germany to the world. People all over the world could not believe that a government could do such horrible acts against its people. The Nazis, who were captured after the end of WWII, were tried and convicted for crimes against humanity. They were executed or imprisoned.

Key Words

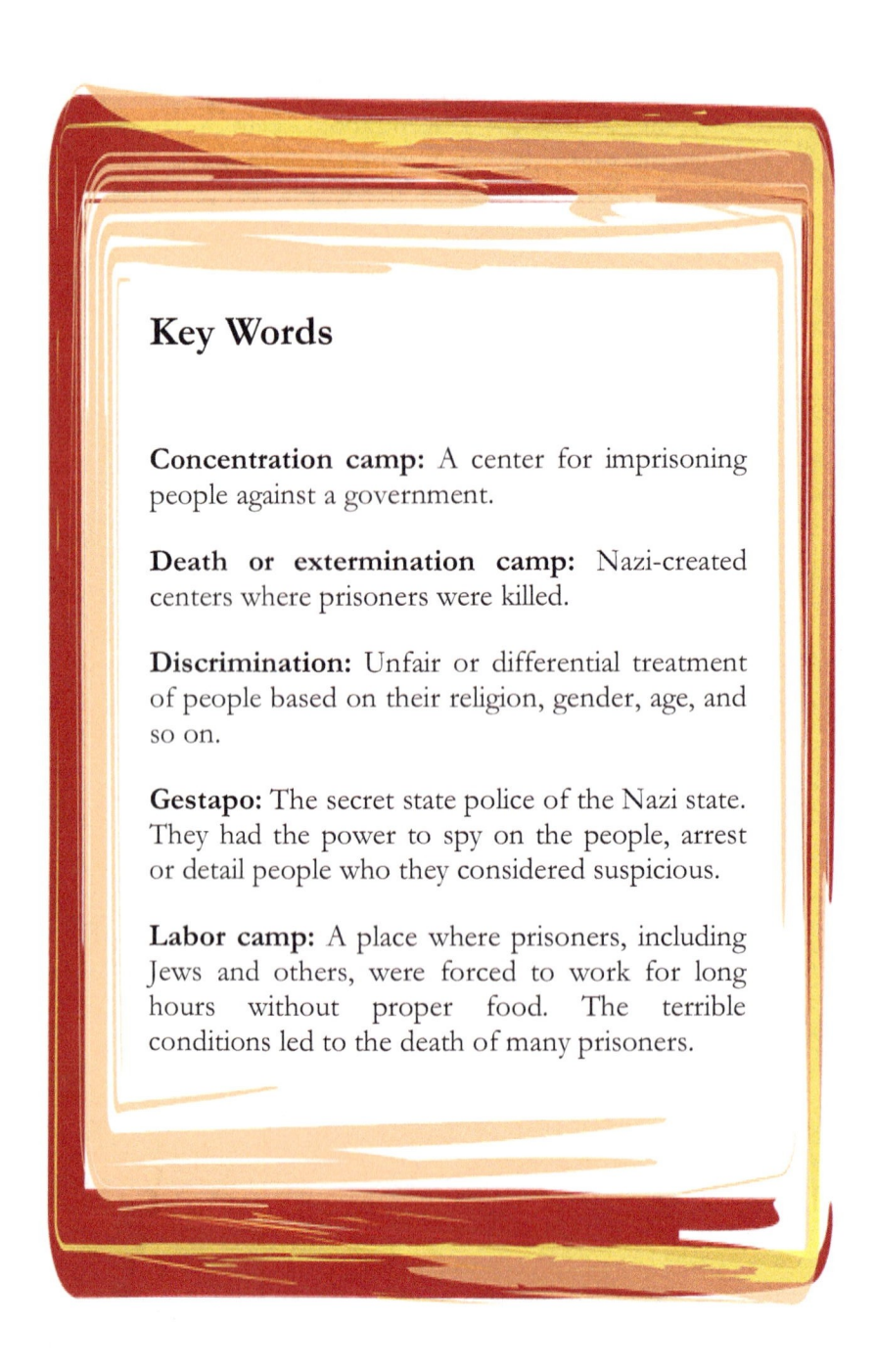

Concentration camp: A center for imprisoning people against a government.

Death or extermination camp: Nazi-created centers where prisoners were killed.

Discrimination: Unfair or differential treatment of people based on their religion, gender, age, and so on.

Gestapo: The secret state police of the Nazi state. They had the power to spy on the people, arrest or detail people who they considered suspicious.

Labor camp: A place where prisoners, including Jews and others, were forced to work for long hours without proper food. The terrible conditions led to the death of many prisoners.

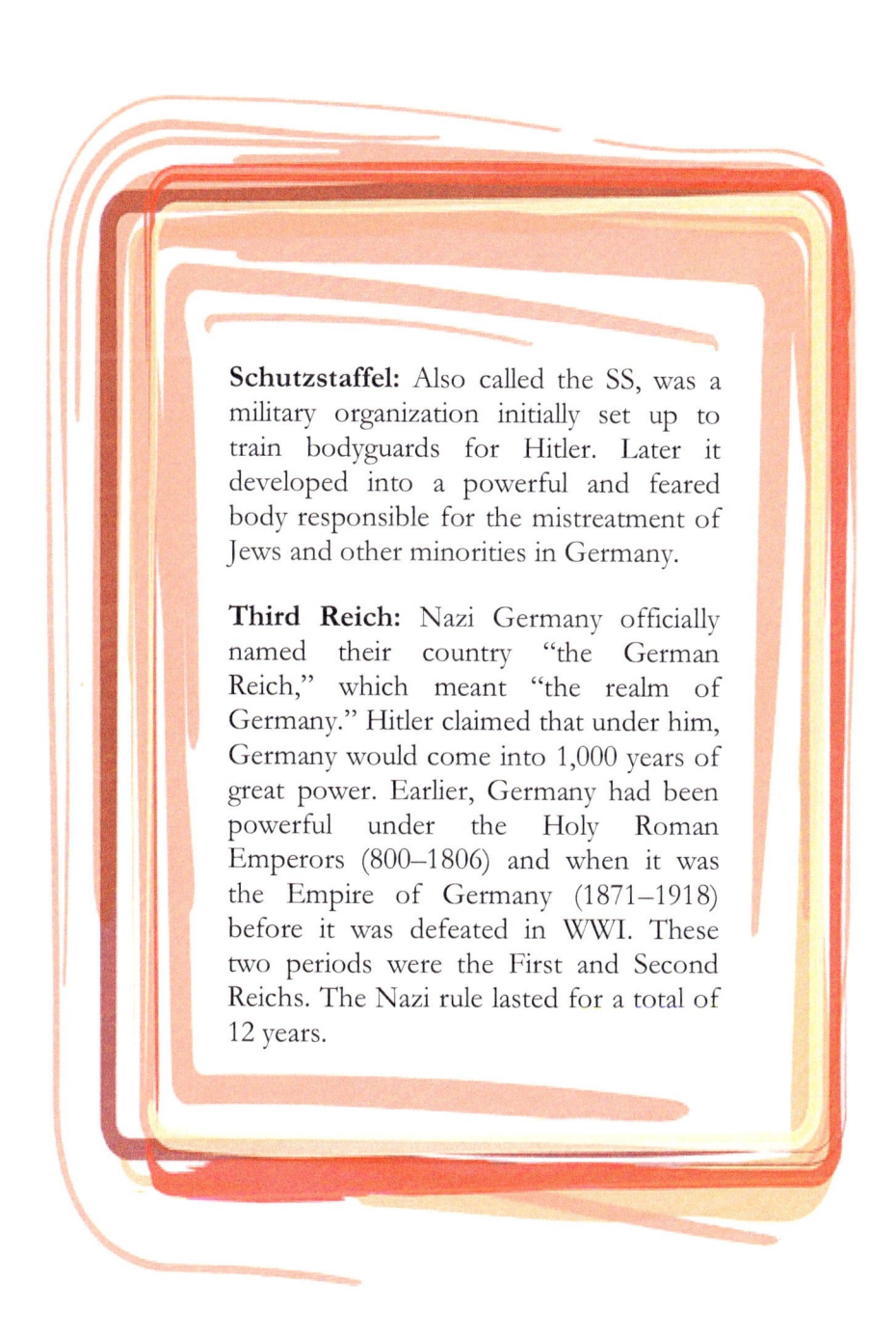

Schutzstaffel: Also called the SS, was a military organization initially set up to train bodyguards for Hitler. Later it developed into a powerful and feared body responsible for the mistreatment of Jews and other minorities in Germany.

Third Reich: Nazi Germany officially named their country "the German Reich," which meant "the realm of Germany." Hitler claimed that under him, Germany would come into 1,000 years of great power. Earlier, Germany had been powerful under the Holy Roman Emperors (800–1806) and when it was the Empire of Germany (1871–1918) before it was defeated in WWI. These two periods were the First and Second Reichs. The Nazi rule lasted for a total of 12 years.

Quiz

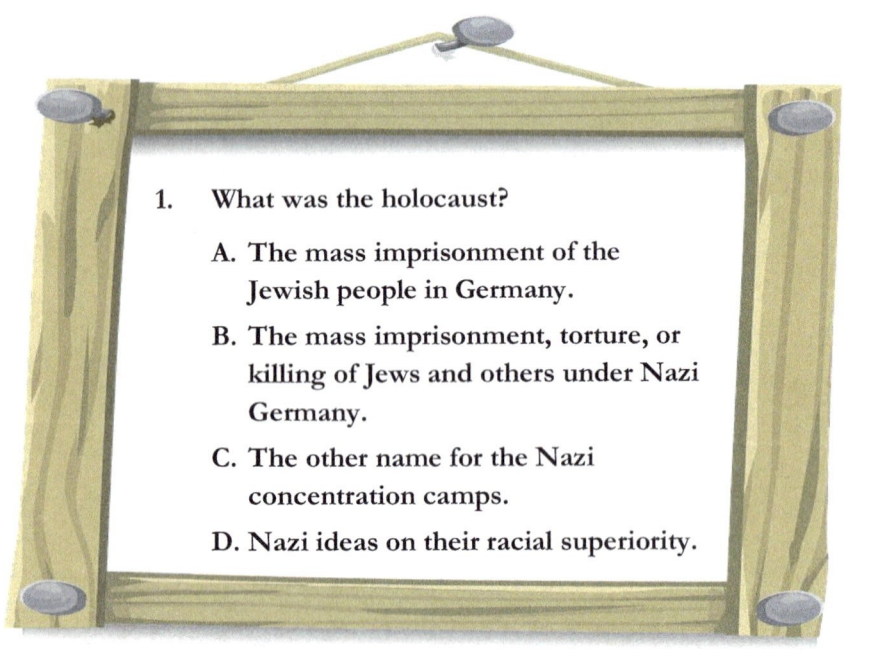

1. What was the holocaust?

   A. The mass imprisonment of the Jewish people in Germany.

   B. The mass imprisonment, torture, or killing of Jews and others under Nazi Germany.

   C. The other name for the Nazi concentration camps.

   D. Nazi ideas on their racial superiority.

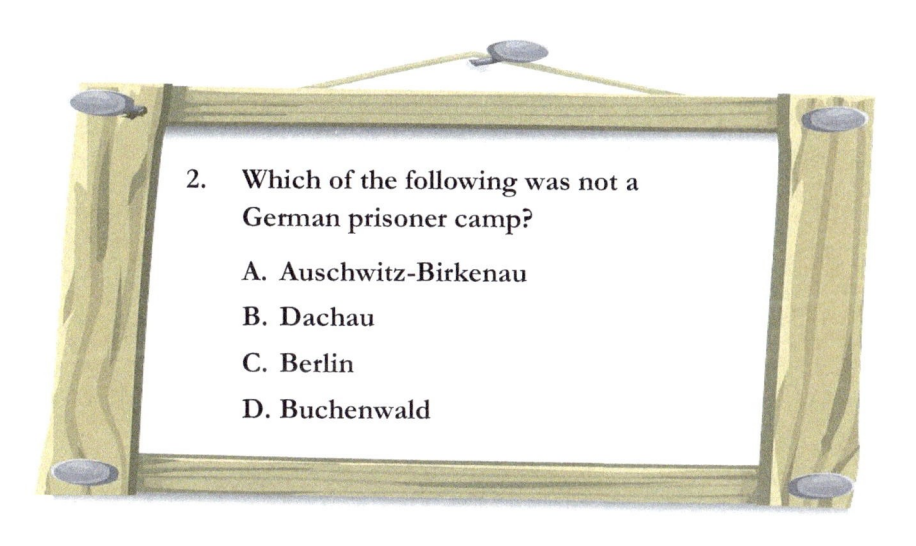

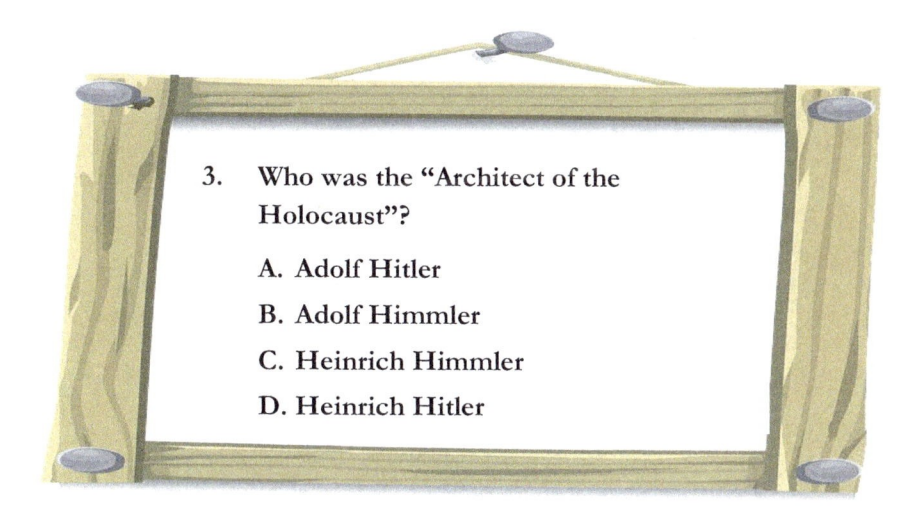

2. Which of the following was not a German prisoner camp?

   A. Auschwitz-Birkenau

   B. Dachau

   C. Berlin

   D. Buchenwald

3. Who was the "Architect of the Holocaust"?

   A. Adolf Hitler

   B. Adolf Himmler

   C. Heinrich Himmler

   D. Heinrich Hitler

4. The first prisoner camp to be liberated was _____.

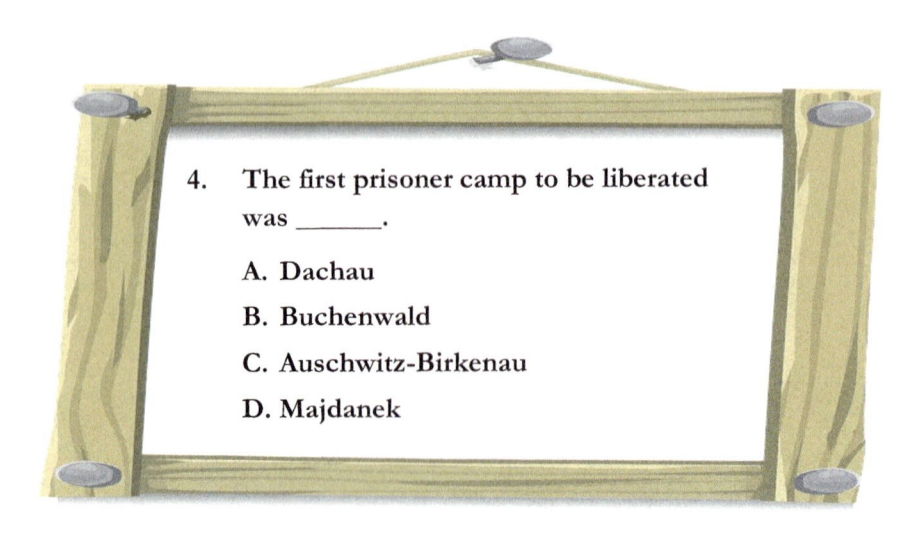

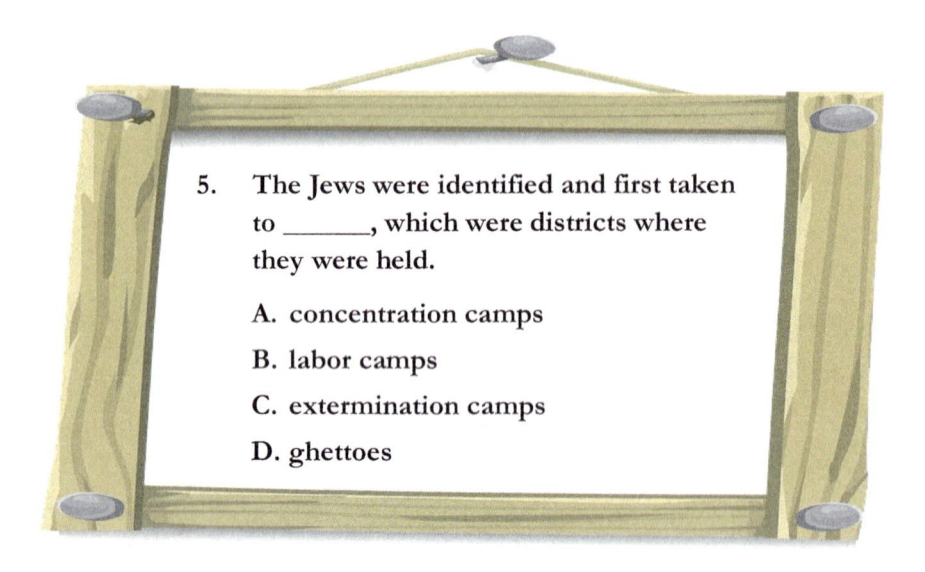

   A. Dachau
   B. Buchenwald
   C. Auschwitz-Birkenau
   D. Majdanek

5. The Jews were identified and first taken to _____, which were districts where they were held.

   A. concentration camps
   B. labor camps
   C. extermination camps
   D. ghettoes

Chapter 12:

In Berlin at the End of the War

Berlin's Surrender and the Two V-Days

Tim and Maya heard the news of Hitler's death on the radio broadcast of some friendly soldiers in Weimar. This was on April 30, 1945. Immediately, they used the clock and left for Berlin. But they chose a date, a little after his death—the 10th of May. The children knew this would most likely take them to the final scenes of the war.

When they reached Berlin, it was a sad state indeed. The once glorious capital of Germany was reduced to a pile of rubble. Though Tim and Maya knew this was "enemy" territory, the ruins of houses and public buildings—blown apart, burnt down, and destroyed, filled their hearts with pity rather than joy. People here had suffered and struggled too. Now they, like others all over Europe, would have years ahead of them in which cities, lives, and homes would have to be rebuilt.

What an absolute mess a war made! There was nothing glorious, brave, or freeing about war—not for the Allies or the Axis. All across the world now, the people who survived would live in sadness for the loved ones they lost. They would need to pick up the pieces as best as they could. If only Hitler could see the beloved capital of his beloved country now, would he still have decided to start the war? The children felt sad and had doubts as they walked through the city.

The ordinary people of Berlin seemed to be just relieved that the bombing and air raids had stopped. Most of them were shifting piles of bricks to find if there was somebody still alive and trapped beneath it. The children saw civilians waving white flags or handkerchiefs at Allied soldiers. Tim and Maya frequently saw US, Soviet, and British soldiers walking around and trying to maintain law and order as best as they could.

From some soldiers, they learned of the final battle of WWII—the Battle of Berlin, which lasted only a few days, from April 20 to May 2, 1945. After Hitler's death, the fighting continued for only two more days, until the German side understood the pointlessness of it. Berlin was overrun with Russian and Allied soldiers.

In the presence of Eisenhower's chief of staff and a Soviet general, the German General Alfred Jodl formally signed their surrender in Reims, a city in France. The document clearly stated that all German forces would stop fighting on May 8, 1945.

However, the Soviets, who had lost more at the hands of Germany, weren't satisfied. They wanted the Nazis to sign another treaty with their Red Army. German Field Marshal Wilhelm Keitel signed this in the presence of General Georgi Zhukov, the commander-in-chief of the Soviet army, in Berlin on May 8th. This surrender was dated one day later, on May 9th.

So, while Western Europe celebrated V-Day on May 8th, the Soviets celebrated it on May 9th. Tim and Maya understood that this was why there were two V-Days even now. The one in Europe is also called Victory in Europe Day or VE-Day, while the other is simply called Victory Day (V-Day).

The Last Days of the Dictator

Tim and Maya also learned more about Adolf Hitler. People were now more willing to talk about the man. The children understood that not every German had agreed with or known of Hitler's plans. Many of them had joined the Nazis only to keep their own families safe. In fact, many of the common citizens were shocked by the reports of the Jewish concentration camps.

From soldiers' reports, the children pieced together Hitler's last days. He, his long-time girlfriend, Eva Braun, and some of his most trusted ministers retired to the Führerbunker sometime in January 1945. This place was the air raid shelters he had built for himself under his official home or the Reich Chancellery in Berlin.

The Führer or Leader, as Hitler styled himself, knew that the end was near. He had always refused to marry because he claimed his country took importance over his personal life. But maybe because he knew the end was near, he quietly married Eva Braun. The Hitlers were only married for a few days, though. Meanwhile, reports of Germany's defeat were pouring in. Though many of his ministers begged him to issue the order for German surrender, Hitler wanted Berlin to fight to the end.

On the day of his death, after eating his last meal with some of his staff, shaking hands, and thanking all the others around him, the couple retired to their room. Hitler committed suicide by shooting himself, while Eva Braun bit on a cyanide pill to end her life. He even had their pet dogs put down. Hitler had already given instructions for his wife and himself to be buried outside the Führerbunker to his trusted staff members, who dutifully completed this task.

After his death and the fall of the Reich, many Nazis fled and remained in hiding; some killed themselves and their families, while others who were caught were executed or imprisoned.

Tim and Maya knew in their hearts that a headless Germany was far from peace. They felt sad for the people, while also feeling happy that the fighting had stopped.

Berlin's Fall and Germany's Partition

In the days after the Nazi rule ended, it was clear to the Allies that Germany needed as much help with rebuilding itself as other European countries.

The whole of Germany and Berlin was divided into four administrative zones under the US, UK, France, and Soviet Union. Eventually, the first three zones joined to form West Germany or the Federal Republic of Germany, while East Germany, under Soviet control, became the German Democratic Republic in 1949. Germany thus became two countries as political problems between the US and the Soviet Union increased.

Do You Know?

When Germany fell, the Allies fought among themselves not just to rule over Germany and for world power but also to divide up the best brains of the Reich. German scientists, mathematicians, and other minds were given irresistible offers to emigrate and join teams in the US, UK, France, and Russia. This was another point of tension between the communist Russians and the capitalist Allies.

Key Words

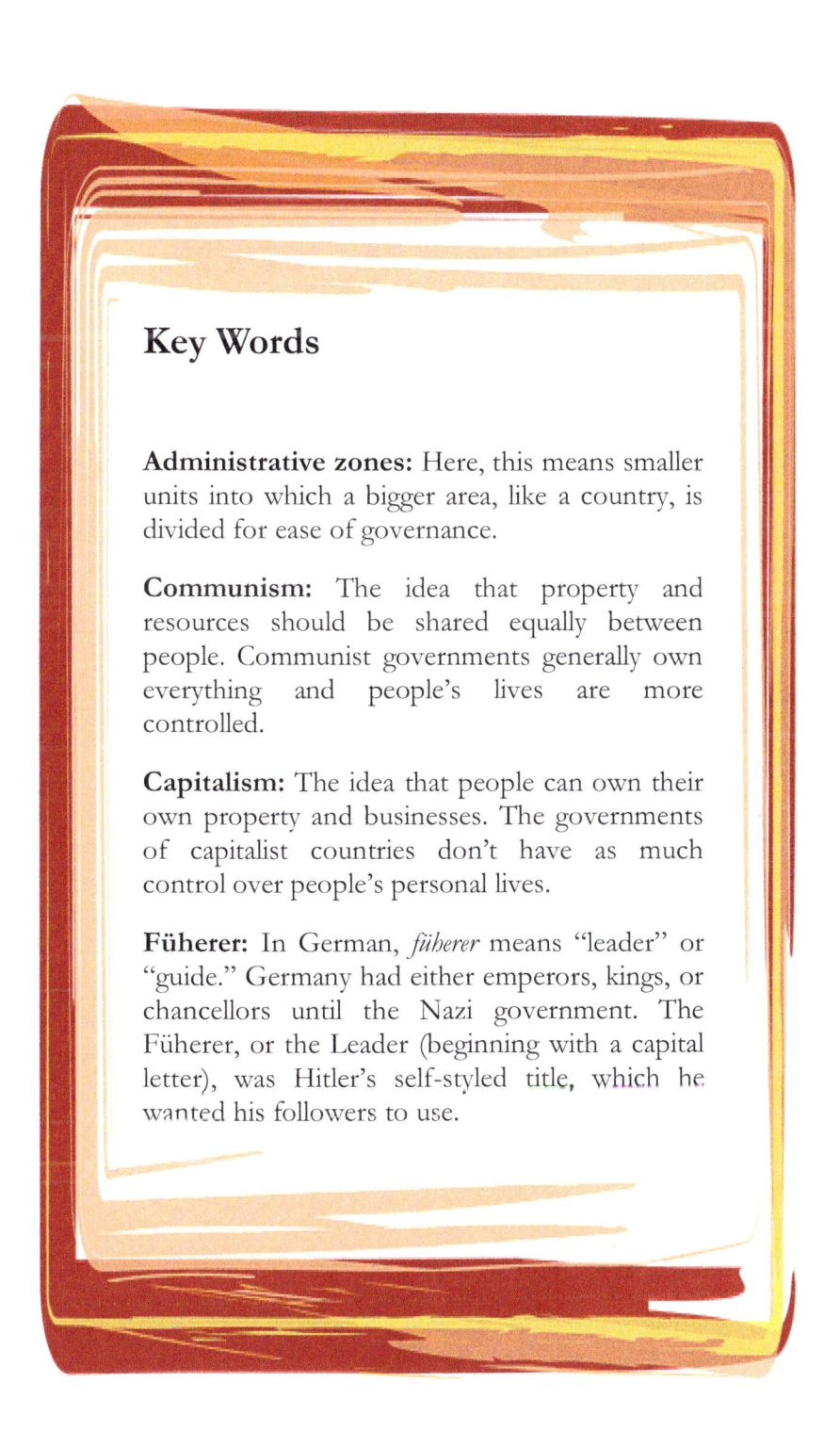

Administrative zones: Here, this means smaller units into which a bigger area, like a country, is divided for ease of governance.

Communism: The idea that property and resources should be shared equally between people. Communist governments generally own everything and people's lives are more controlled.

Capitalism: The idea that people can own their own property and businesses. The governments of capitalist countries don't have as much control over people's personal lives.

Führer: In German, *führer* means "leader" or "guide." Germany had either emperors, kings, or chancellors until the Nazi government. The Führer, or the Leader (beginning with a capital letter), was Hitler's self-styled title, which he wanted his followers to use.

Quiz

1. Victory Day in Western Europe was on _____.

    A. April 30, 1945
    B. May 7, 1945
    C. May 8, 1945
    D. May 9, 1945

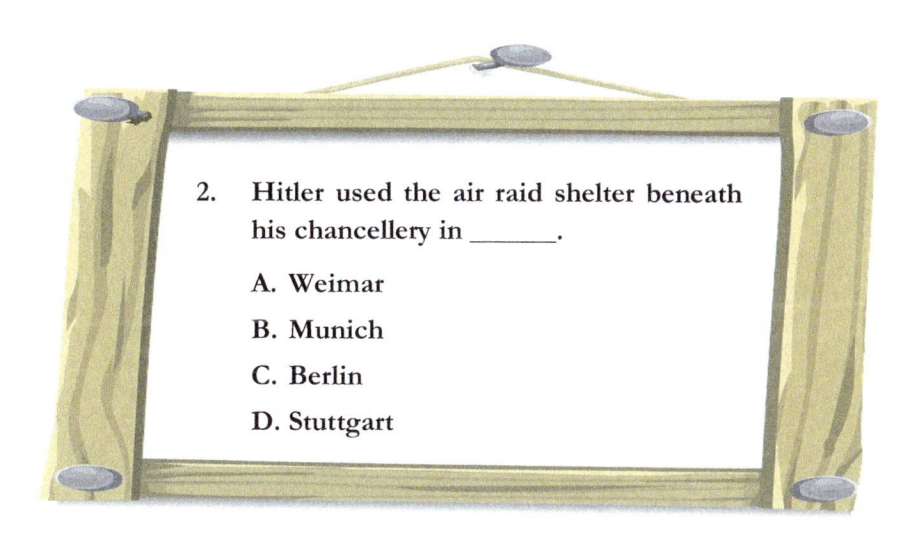

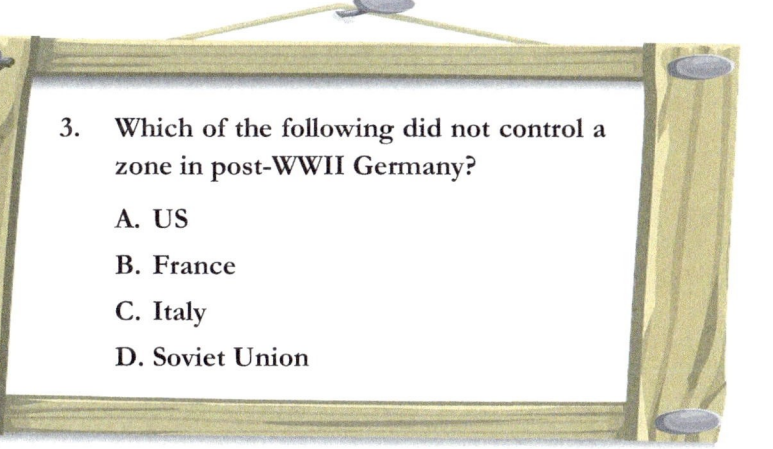

2. Hitler used the air raid shelter beneath his chancellery in _____.

   A. Weimar
   B. Munich
   C. Berlin
   D. Stuttgart

3. Which of the following did not control a zone in post-WWII Germany?

   A. US
   B. France
   C. Italy
   D. Soviet Union

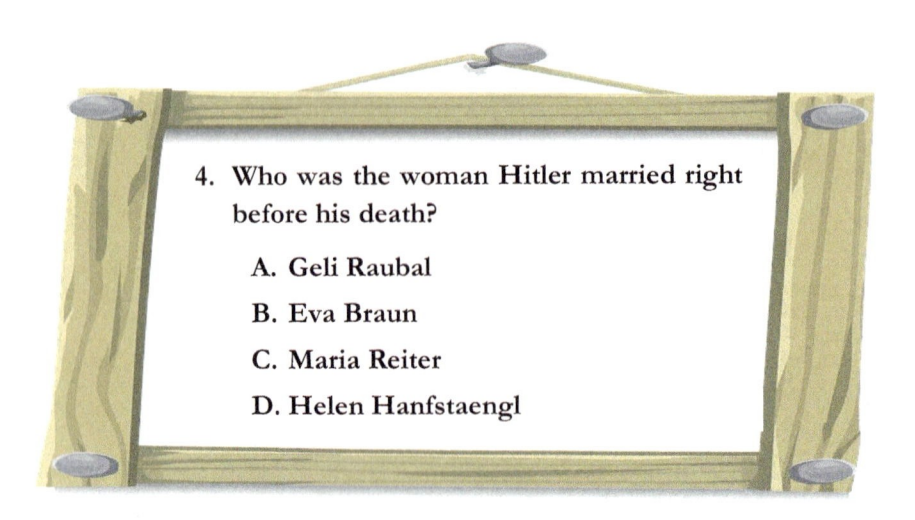

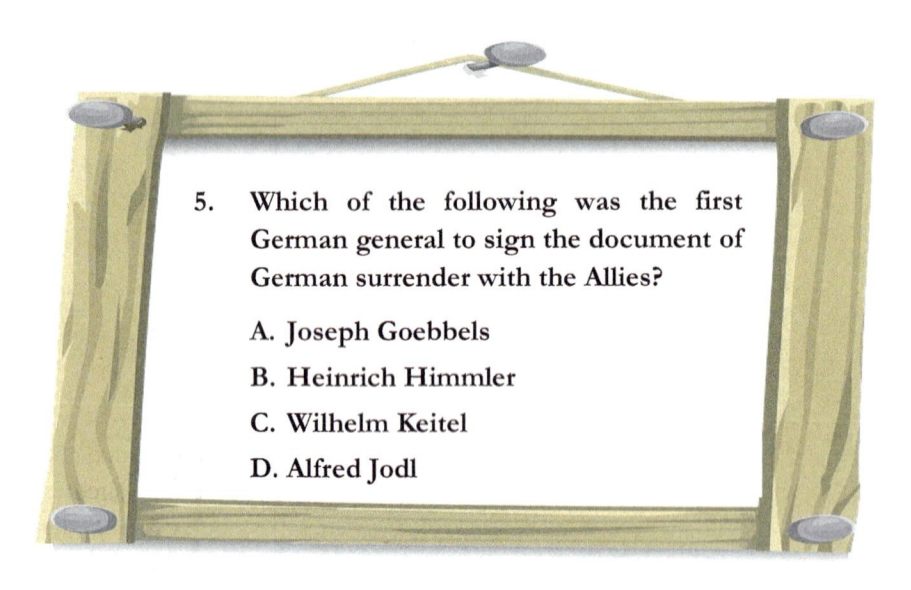

4. Who was the woman Hitler married right before his death?

   A. Geli Raubal

   B. Eva Braun

   C. Maria Reiter

   D. Helen Hanfstaengl

5. Which of the following was the first German general to sign the document of German surrender with the Allies?

   A. Joseph Goebbels

   B. Heinrich Himmler

   C. Wilhelm Keitel

   D. Alfred Jodl

Chapter 13:

The Manhattan Project

The Secret Project—Manhattan Project

Tim and Maya wanted to know what happened in Japan that ended the war. They vaguely knew about the Hiroshima and Nagasaki tragedies when the US dropped atomic bombs on the two cities, causing the Japanese to surrender on August 14, 1945. But how and where was this bomb developed?

Tim had some answers. He had wanted to watch the movie, *Oppenheimer*. But their parents told him he needed to be at least 15 years old to watch it. Though disappointed, he had read up on the movie and what it was about.

He told Maya, "I know! We can go to Los Alamos and meet the people behind the Manhattan Project!"

Maya, who did not follow war movies, did not know what Tim was talking about. But she trusted Tim's deep interest in the subject and followed his lead.

The scientists in the US had been working hard on a secret project called the Manhattan Project. It aimed to develop an atomic bomb. This project was so hush-hush that only the U.S. President and a few people on the team knew of its existence. The work, divided into three parts, was being carried out not just at Los Alamos but also at Hanford in California and Oak Ridge in Tennessee.

Los Alamos—Project Y

The clock took them to Los Alamos in New Mexico in July 1945.

At Los Alamos, the work on Project Y of the Manhattan Project was slowly coming to an end. The scientists were about to test-fire the atomic bomb in the deserts for the first time in US history—the Trinity Nuclear Test.

Los Alamos did not look like a big laboratory as the children imagined. The scientists had brought their families along during their work. It was a settlement camp in the desert, where there were homes, schools, and everything you could expect and want in a small town.

Tim and Maya hung back with the other children in the camp and waited for news of the results. From them, Tim and Maya understood the camp had been working since 1943. Very soon, they heard that the testing was a success. When the men returned, they walked around till they heard more about the people behind the project.

The People

Tim and Maya briefly saw one thin man in a hat and suit being congratulated by all. Everyone was shaking hands with him, clapping him on the back, and affectionately calling him "Oppie." Asking one of the other children, they learned this was Robert J. Oppenheimer, the man behind the success of the Trinity and the Director of Project Y. Tim thought that if an entire Christopher Nolan movie had to be taken around this man and his project, then he really must have been historically important. *It is no wonder*, Maya thought, *he is called the Father of the Atomic Bomb.*

The other man the children saw around a lot was Brigadier General Leslie R. Groves Jr. The president had appointed him to be the Director of the entire Manhattan Project. Tim and Maya realized what a stressful job he must have had in coordinating and overseeing the whole project, happening at three different, far-away places in the country!

Tim and Maya saw that though the scientists were happy, having successfully completed a job they were given, some of them looked very troubled. Tim remembered how some scientists who worked on the project would later try to hand over a petition to the government pleading with leaders not to use the bomb on Japan. The scientists knew nuclear power was a weapon that could wipe out entire cities and families. Tim and Maya correctly guessed that these were the thoughts and doubts most of the scientists at Los Alamos were going through.

The development of the atomic bomb led to the development of the hydrogen bomb, a weapon that Oppenheimer felt needed to be researched but hoped would never be built. Later in life, he was one of the people who actively spoke against nuclear weapons.

History tells us how the US government dropped the bombs on Hiroshima on August 6 and Nagasaki on August 9, 1945. Japan had no choice but to surrender. Though the war ended, these two days are among the blackest in human history! So powerful was the radiation of these two bombs that many of the survivors died from health complications like cancer later on in their lives.

Do You Know?

- Albert Einstein and Leo Szilard were the two scientists who mainly wrote the letter in 1939 to President Roosevelt to start the American nuclear program because they feared the Germans were already working on it. Einstein and Szilard, who were both Jews, had fled from Germany around the time the Nazis came into power. Einstein was not given the security clearance to work on the Manhattan Project because he had communist leanings.

- President Franklin D. Roosevelt died of a cardiac arrest in April 1945 and was replaced by President Harry S. Truman, who had been the Vice President until then. President Truman only learned about the Manhattan Project after he became president. He authorized the dropping of the bombs on Japan to end WWII.

- The two bombs were nicknamed "Little Boy" and "Fat Man." Little Boy, dropped on Hiroshima, was smaller and used uranium as fuel, while Fat Man, dropped on Nagasaki, was bigger and heavier and fueled by plutonium. Fat Man was 10 times stronger than Little Boy.

Key Words

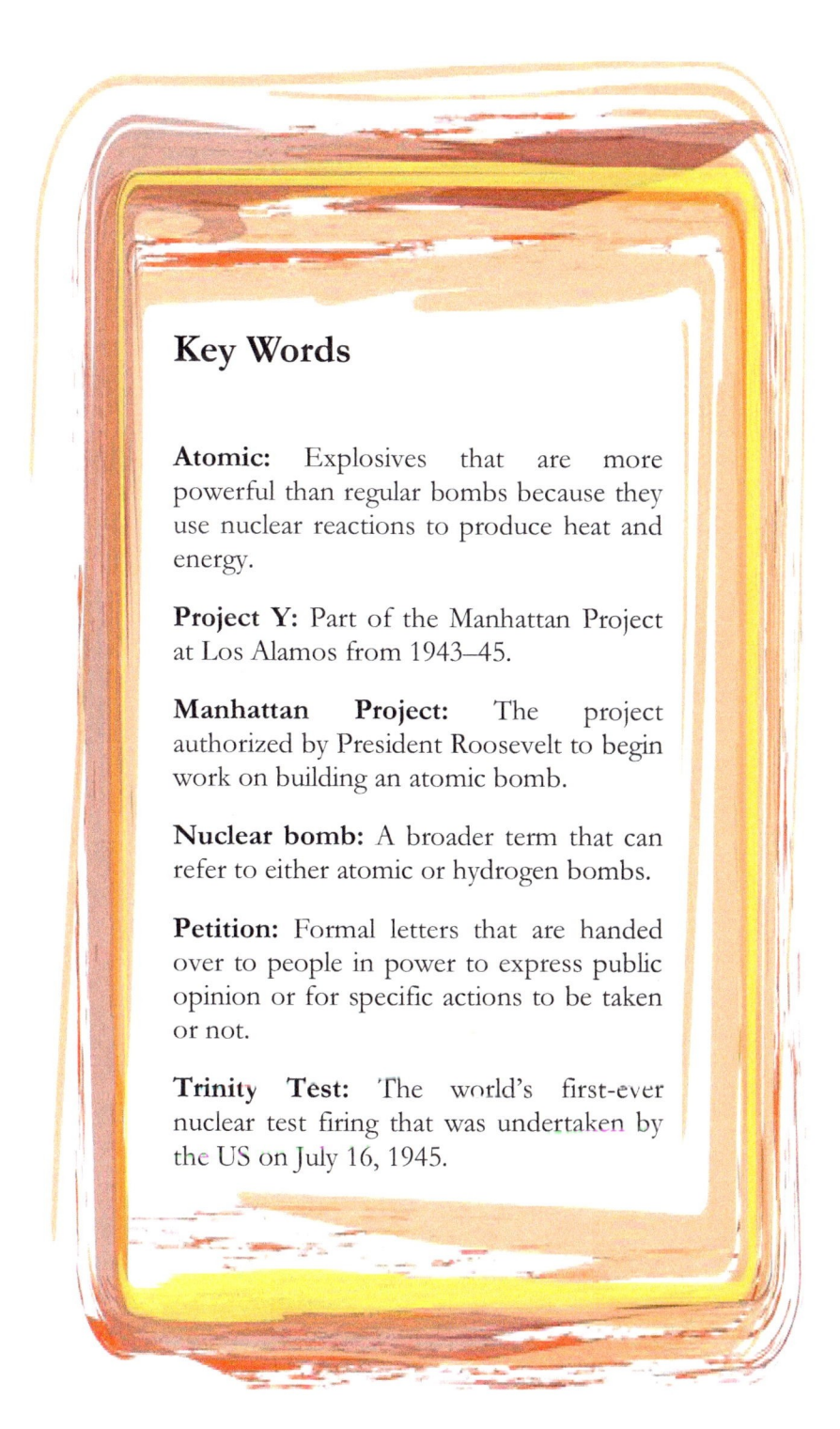

Atomic: Explosives that are more powerful than regular bombs because they use nuclear reactions to produce heat and energy.

Project Y: Part of the Manhattan Project at Los Alamos from 1943–45.

Manhattan Project: The project authorized by President Roosevelt to begin work on building an atomic bomb.

Nuclear bomb: A broader term that can refer to either atomic or hydrogen bombs.

Petition: Formal letters that are handed over to people in power to express public opinion or for specific actions to be taken or not.

Trinity Test: The world's first-ever nuclear test firing that was undertaken by the US on July 16, 1945.

Quiz

1. Who is the Father of the Atomic Bomb?

   A. Leslie Groves
   B. Harry S Truman
   C. Robert J. Oppenheimer
   D. Leo Szilard

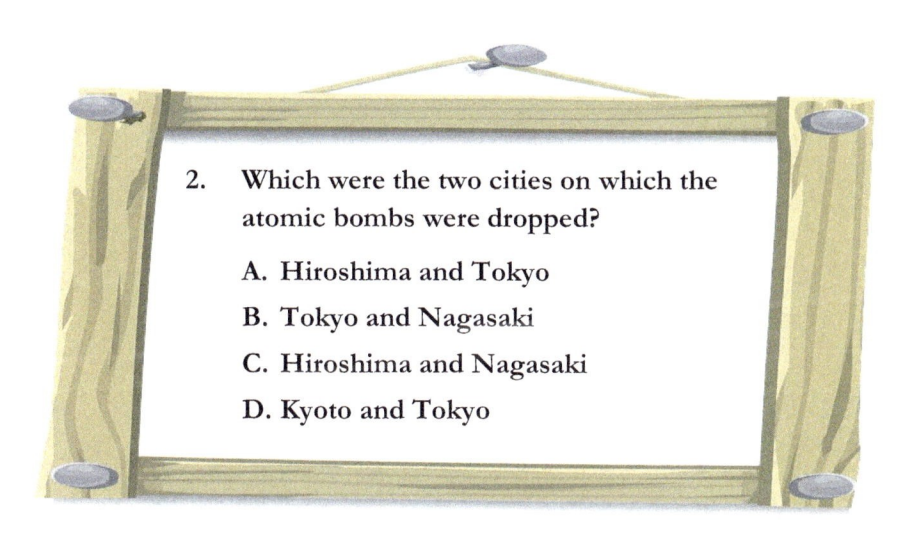

2. Which were the two cities on which the atomic bombs were dropped?

   A. Hiroshima and Tokyo
   B. Tokyo and Nagasaki
   C. Hiroshima and Nagasaki
   D. Kyoto and Tokyo

3. Which U.S. President agreed to the dropping of the Atomic bomb?

   A. President Roosevelt
   B. President Churchill
   C. President de Gaulle
   D. President Truman

4. Who was the director of the Manhattan Project?

   A. Robert Oppenheimer
   B. Brigadier General Leslie R. Groves Jr.
   C. Joseph Stalin
   D. Franklin D. Roosevelt

5. What did the dropping of the two atomic bombs mean for the Second World War?

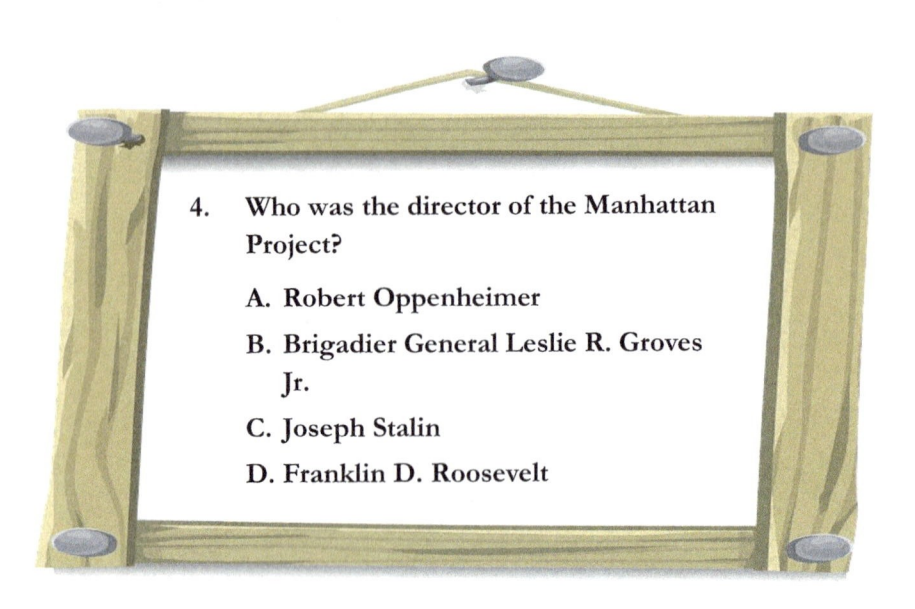

   A. It ensured Germany's surrender, ending the war.
   B. It ensured Italy's surrender, ending the war.
   C. It ensured Russia's surrender, ending the war.
   D. It ensured Japan's surrender, ending the war.

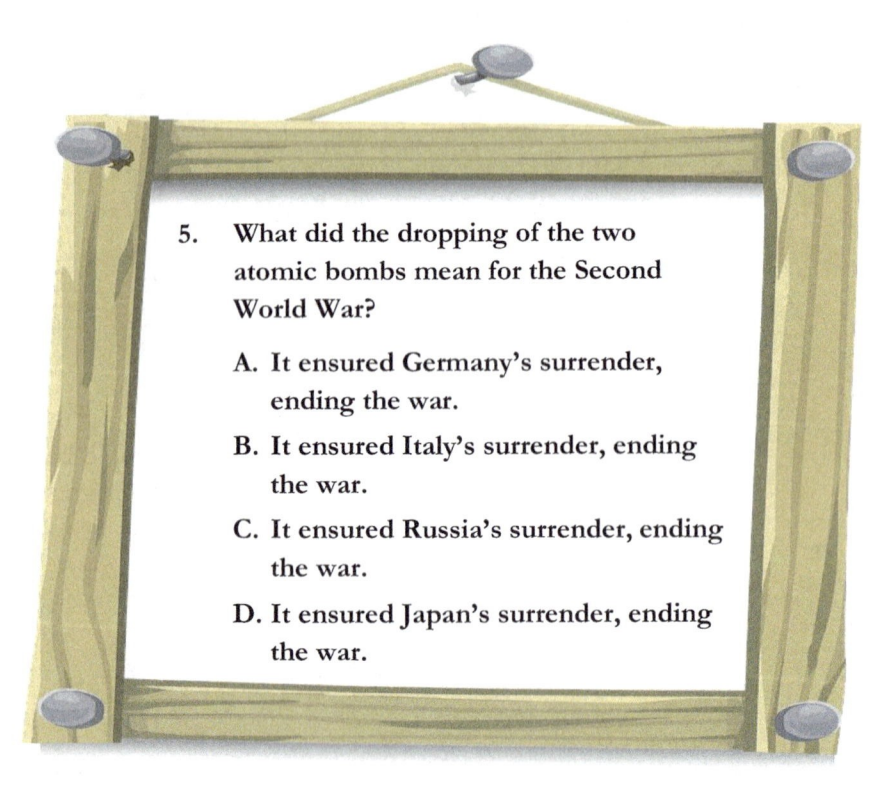

Chapter 14:

The Cold War Begins

The Cold War (1950–1990)

Tim and Maya were still curious about how things ended in Germany. They decided to visit Berlin in 1948 to see how the situation had improved from 1945. The clock took them to the city.

The city they now saw was better developed than the ruins they saw earlier. Even so, one thing bothered them. It seemed that there were two Berlins now. East Berlin was under the Soviets, while West Berlin was under the Allied Powers. The complications were heightened by the onset of the Cold War, a period of escalating tension between the US and the USSR, which was now influencing global politics. There were more complications as Berlin, being deep within the borders of East Germany, made West Berlin a tiny, isolated piece of land governed by the Allies. The two halves of the city were separated by a guarded border line.

Tim and Maya, who had landed in West Berlin, saw that people had built up their lives along the American and British ideas of progress. They met Allied soldiers and vehicles, reminding them and the people that Germany was still "occupied land." However, people were out on the streets doing things like attending school, going to work, shopping, and eating at public restaurants. Life was slowly normalizing.

Tim and Maya met a couple of students who had escaped from East Berlin into the West. They sang a very different tune about life across the border.

One student who could speak English told them, "You won't believe it is the same city across the border. The Soviet Union controls and monitors people closely. Nobody is allowed to do anything without police or armed men asking you for passes or ID frequently. People are punished for following a religion because communism is against religion. Supermarkets, run by the government, have only a few types of food from which people can choose. There are no restaurants or theaters because private citizens aren't allowed to own businesses. We hear Russian is being made compulsory in schools there. And because East Berlin is the seat of the USSR in Germany, it is better than other cities. Other cities in East Germany are far worse because even basic infrastructure, like public transport, is not functioning properly."

Tim and Maya could not take in all this. Of course, they could see why the world powers were so worried and felt they needed to keep Germany in check so that another evil political power like Nazism wouldn't rise again. However, they could also see how the growing Cold War between the USA and the USSR was already beginning to affect the very unity of Germany.

There was one more thing they wanted to witness. They used the clock to land in Washington, D.C., in 1949.

NATO

The North Atlantic Treaty Organization (NATO) was signed in Washington, D.C., on April 4, 1949. Russia was excluded from being a member. NATO was intended to be a group of countries that would fight for world peace and justice.

The children saw the representatives of the 12 member states at the signing in the Departmental Auditorium in D.C. They were seated on a stage as President Truman delivered a speech on world peace.

Asking around, Tim discovered the other countries part of NATO were Canada, the UK, France, Italy, Belgium, Denmark, Iceland, the Netherlands, Norway, Luxembourg, and Portugal. These countries promised to protect each other in case of any future world crisis.

The children finally understood the "Iron Curtain"—the ideology that separated the Western Bloc, led by the US, from the Eastern Bloc of communist countries, led by the USSR, which included Albania, Bulgaria, Hungary, Poland, and Romania.

Maya said, "Now I see why they called this the Cold War. There isn't a war as such, but people are divided anyway."

Tim could only nod in agreement.

Do You Know?

- The Cold War between the US and USSR became so bad that the Soviets blockaded West Berlin between 1948 and 1949. Joseph Stalin, Premier of the USSR, cut off all transportation between West Germany and West Berlin. The Allied countries had to airdrop food and other supplies to West Berlin. By 1949, Germany became two countries—the Federal Republic of Germany, or West Germany, and the German Democratic Republic, or East Germany. West Germany was a democracy with an elected government, while East Germany continued to be controlled by Russia. The two Germanys reunited in 1990, just before the fall of the USSR in 1991.

- The USSR also built the Berlin Wall in 1961, a concrete separation dividing East and West Berlin and going all around West Berlin to separate it from East Germany. This wall was eventually torn down in 1989.

- During the Cold War, the closest the world came to an actual war was the Cuban Missile Crisis. The Soviets installed missiles and weapons in communist Cuba in 1962 to attack the US. After two weeks of heated political talks, Russia removed its weapons, but not before receiving a promise from the US that America would not invade Cuba.

Key Words

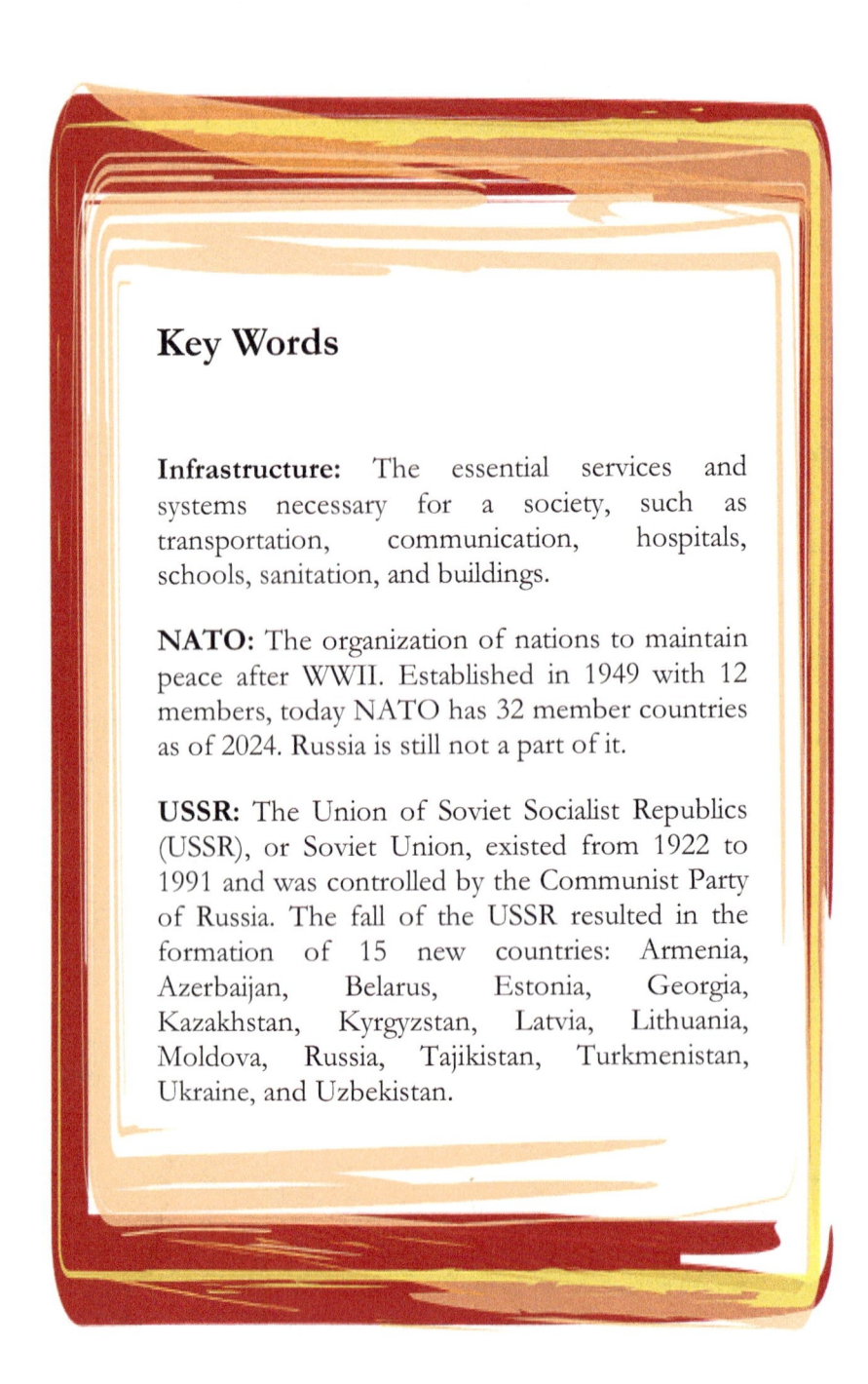

Infrastructure: The essential services and systems necessary for a society, such as transportation, communication, hospitals, schools, sanitation, and buildings.

NATO: The organization of nations to maintain peace after WWII. Established in 1949 with 12 members, today NATO has 32 member countries as of 2024. Russia is still not a part of it.

USSR: The Union of Soviet Socialist Republics (USSR), or Soviet Union, existed from 1922 to 1991 and was controlled by the Communist Party of Russia. The fall of the USSR resulted in the formation of 15 new countries: Armenia, Azerbaijan, Belarus, Estonia, Georgia, Kazakhstan, Kyrgyzstan, Latvia, Lithuania, Moldova, Russia, Tajikistan, Turkmenistan, Ukraine, and Uzbekistan.

Quiz

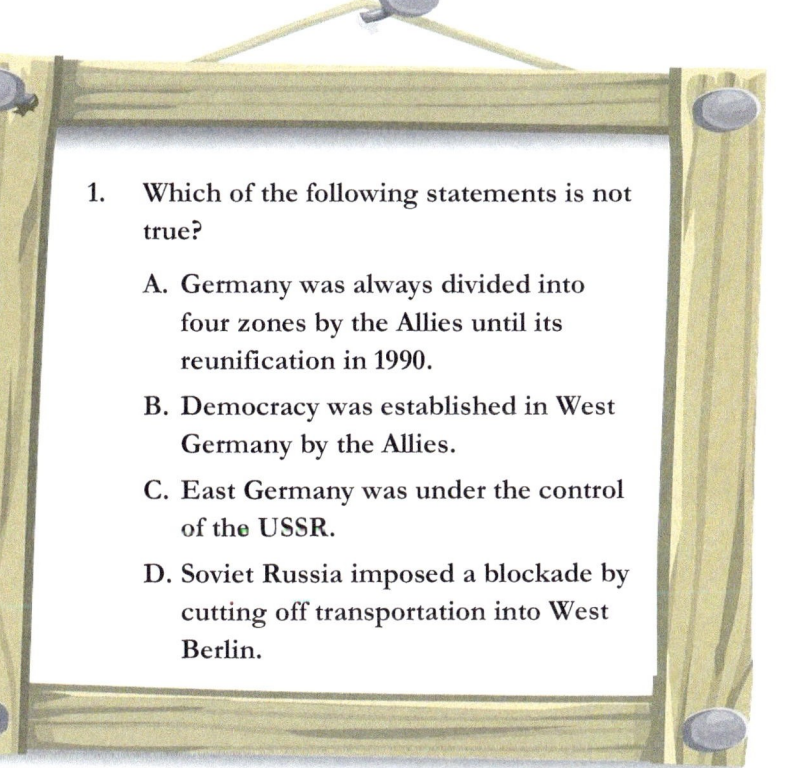

1. Which of the following statements is not true?

    A. Germany was always divided into four zones by the Allies until its reunification in 1990.

    B. Democracy was established in West Germany by the Allies.

    C. East Germany was under the control of the USSR.

    D. Soviet Russia imposed a blockade by cutting off transportation into West Berlin.

2. Who was the Premier of Soviet Russia?

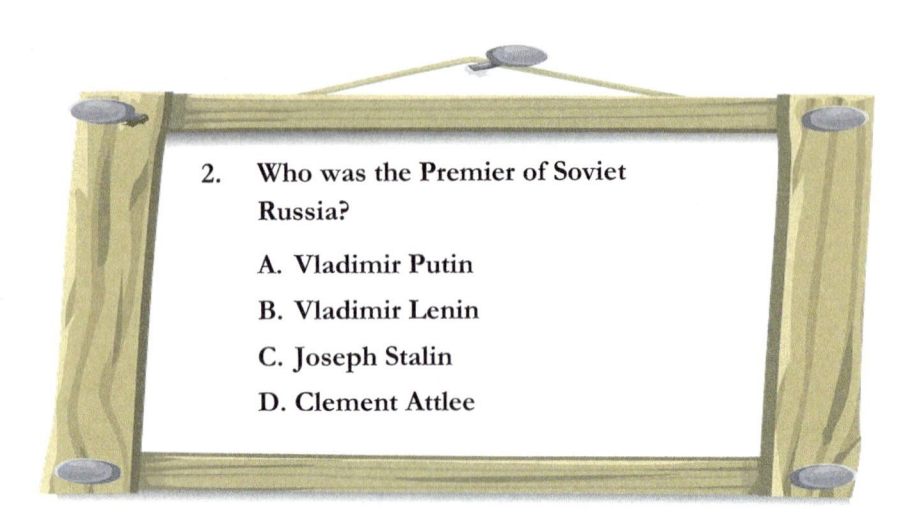

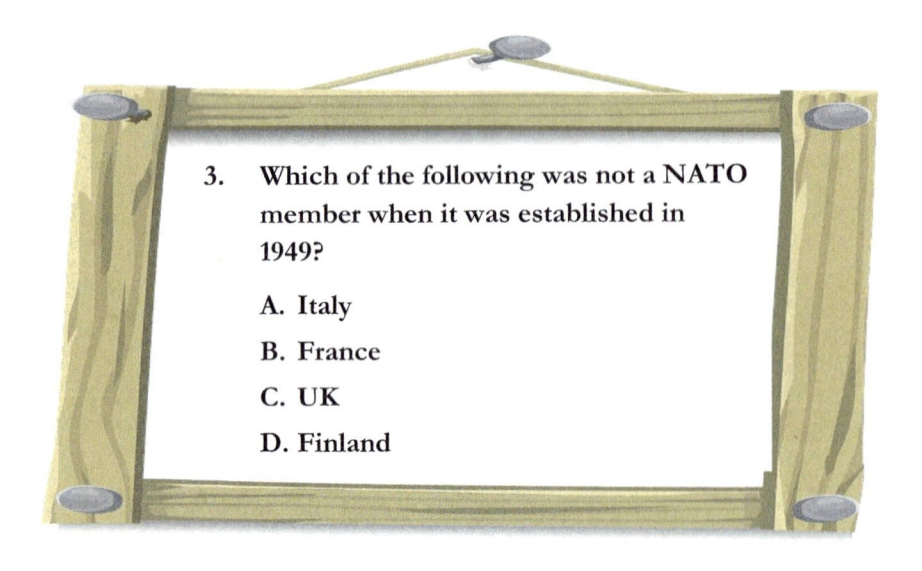

   A. Vladimir Putin
   B. Vladimir Lenin
   C. Joseph Stalin
   D. Clement Attlee

3. Which of the following was not a NATO member when it was established in 1949?

   A. Italy
   B. France
   C. UK
   D. Finland

4. The "Iron Curtain" was the _____.

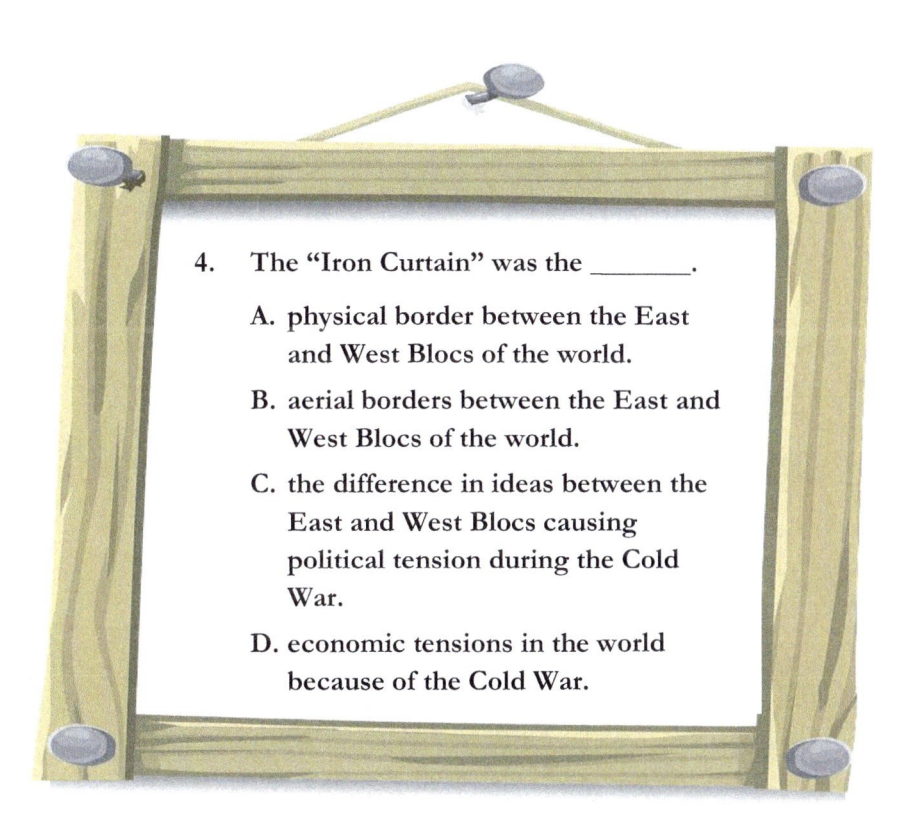

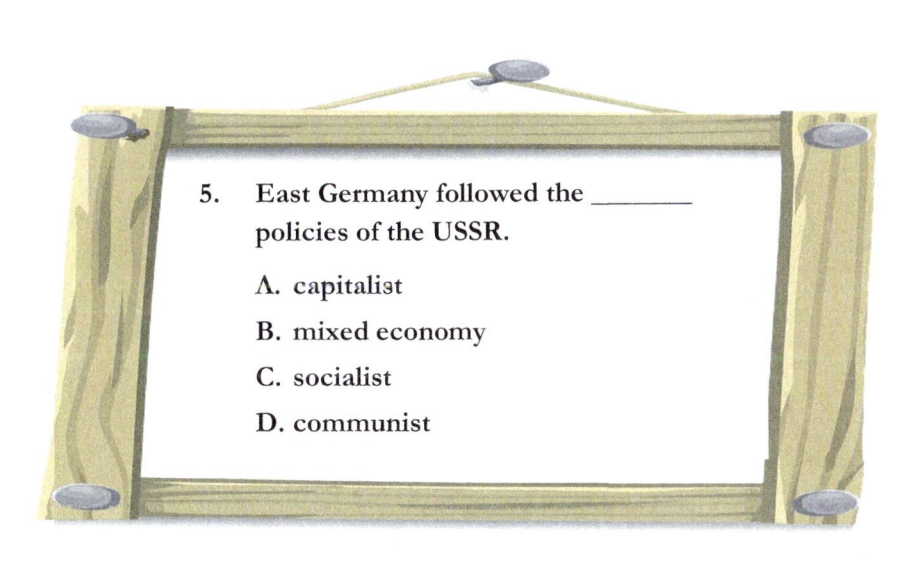

   A. physical border between the East and West Blocs of the world.
   B. aerial borders between the East and West Blocs of the world.
   C. the difference in ideas between the East and West Blocs causing political tension during the Cold War.
   D. economic tensions in the world because of the Cold War.

5. East Germany followed the _____ policies of the USSR.

   A. capitalist
   B. mixed economy
   C. socialist
   D. communist

Chapter 15:

Back to the Present

Time's Running Out

Tim and Maya had seen all that they possibly could. The letters in their pockets were smaller than two small playing cards. If they did not get back to their own home city and timeline now, they might get stuck in the past!

Their only worry now was what their mother would say. They weren't sure if they would land back on the same day as they had left. What if a couple of days had gone by and their mother was worried sick about their whereabouts?

Quickly, for the last time, they closed their eyes and said together, "New York, May 2024." The whoosh and swoop came, and before they could say anything more, they were back in the secret room of the museum.

Back to the Here and Now

They ran out of the room and hurried through the museum's lounge. Just as they were beginning to panic, a familiar voice called out to them, "Tim and Maya! Here!" The children ran into the outstretched arms of their mom.

Tim said, "Sorry. We just got lost and—"

Maya eagerly added, "We saw the most—"

Mother said, "Relax. There is still time." She was pointing at the large clock in the front room of the museum. It was true—the clock read 11:50 a.m. Tim and Maya were amazed. It was as if they had lost no time at all!

In the car to their favorite pizza joint in New York, Tim and Maya debated in whispers whether they should tell their mother about their adventures. They finally decided that nobody would believe them. Their mother least of all. She would just laughingly say that they had found "a new-found interest" in the Second World War and "were exaggerating their learning."

Tim and Maya also thought that telling another person would break the spell. They intended to get back into the clock room of the museum again and test their luck—because why not?

Secretly, their mother watched them in the front mirror of their car. She was pleased Tim and Maya seemed immersed in their discussion of WWII. They weren't even whining for their tablets or laptops.

A New Appreciation

In the next couple of days, Maya ditched all plans to watch her Netflix series, instead borrowing *Anne Frank's Diary* from the local library. Even when Tim used the tablet, he was mostly researching the vehicles and weaponry used during World War II.

Now and then, the children shared stories and anecdotes from the war at the dinner table. Their mother was really very surprised at this transformation in them. She decided she would take them to the museum and library more often!

Meanwhile, in a dark room in an old museum in New York, an old clock waited for Tim and Maya and others like them so that it could carry them through the portals of time!

Historical Notes

A Timeline of Events

1933–1939: Prelude to World War II

- **1933:** Adolf Hitler becomes Chancellor of Germany; Nazi Party gains power.

- **1935:** Nuremberg Laws are enacted, stripping Jews of citizenship in Germany.

- **1936**

    - **March:** Germany remilitarizes against the Treaty of Versailles they signed after their defeat in WWI in 1918.

    - **May:** Italy, under the Fascist dictator Benito Mussolini, completes the conquest of Ethiopia, establishing the Italian East African Empire.

    - **November:** Fascist Italy joins Nazi Germany, signing the Rome-Berlin Axis.

- **1938:** Munich Agreement allows Nazi annexation of the Sudetenland (Czechoslovakia).

- **1939**

    - **March 15:** Germany invades the remainder of Czechoslovakia.

- **April 7:** Italy invades Albania, further expanding its imperialist ambitions.
- **May 22:** Italy and Germany sign the Pact of Steel, solidifying their military alliance.
- **August 23:** Nazi-Soviet Non-Aggression Pact signed.
- **September 1:** Germany invades Poland, triggering World War II. Italy remains neutral initially.
- **September 3:** Britain and France declare war on Germany.

1939–1945: World War II

- 1940

  - **April–June:** Nazi Germany invades Denmark, Norway, Belgium, Netherlands, and France.
  - **June 10:** Italy enters World War II on the Axis side, declaring war on France and Britain.
  - **July–October:** Battle of Britain; Germany fails to achieve air superiority.
  - **September:** Japan joins the Axis Powers by signing the Tripartite Pact with Nazi Germany and Fascist Italy.
  - **October**
    - Japan occupies French Indochina (Vietnam, Laos, Cambodia), escalating tensions with the United States and European colonial powers.
    - Italy invades Greece from Albania, but the campaign stalls and requires German assistance.

- **1941**

    - **April 13:** Japan signs a neutrality pact with the Soviet Union.

    - **June 22:** Germany invades the Soviet Union in Operation Barbarossa. Germany violated the Nazi-Soviet Union Non-Aggression pact, angering the Soviets and their leader, Joseph Stalin.

    - **December 7:** Japan attacks Pearl Harbor; the US enters the war.

- **1942**

    - **January–March:** Japan expands its control over Southeast Asia, capturing the Philippines, Malaya, Singapore, Indonesia, and Burma.

    - The tide of war turns with key Allied victories: e.g., the Battle of Midway (June 4–7, 1942) in the Pacific and the Battle of El Alamein in Africa (October 23–November 11), and others.

- **1943**

    - **February 2:** Germany is defeated in Stalingrad (Volgograd now), Russia.

    - **July 9–10:** Allied forces invade Sicily, Greece, in Operation Husky, marking the beginning of Italy's downfall in the war.

    - **July 25:** Benito Mussolini, the Italian dictator, was captured and arrested by his own country.

    - **September 8:** Italy surrenders to the Allies, although fighting in Italy continues.

    - **September 12:** Mussolini is rescued by German forces and establishes the Italian Social Republic (RSI) in northern Italy under Nazi control.

- 1944
  - **June 6:** D-Day; Allied forces invade Normandy, France.
  - **August 25:** Liberation of Paris by Allied forces.
- 1945
  - **March 9–10:** The U.S. firebombing of Tokyo results in massive civilian casualties.
  - **April**
    - **1:** Battle of Okinawa, Japan begins—one of the bloodiest battles of the Pacific Theater.
    - **28:** Benito Mussolini is captured and murdered by anti-Fascist groups in Italy.
    - **30:** Adolf Hitler commits suicide.
  - **May 7–8:** Germany surrenders to the Allies (V-E Day).
  - **August**
    - **6 and 9:** The US drops atomic bombs on Hiroshima and Nagasaki.
    - **15:** Emperor Hirohito of Japan announces Japan's surrender in a radio broadcast (V-J Day), ending World War II.
  - **September 2:** Official Japanese surrender; Allied occupation of Japan begins

Post-War Era (1945–1950)

- **1945**

  - **July–August:** Potsdam Conference; Allies decide on post-war administration of Germany.

  - **November:** Nuremberg Trials begin to punish Nazi war criminals.

- **1946**

  - **June:** Italy becomes a republic, abolishing monarchy.

- **1947**

  - **May:** Japan, occupied mainly by the US, adopts a new constitution, renouncing war and establishing a parliamentary democracy. The emperor is retained as a symbolic figure with no political power.

  - **June:** The US announces the Marshall Plan to aid European recovery.

- **1948**

  - **June:** Soviet Union's Berlin Blockade begins; Allies launch the Berlin Airlift.

- **1949**

  - **April:** NATO (North Atlantic Treaty Organization) is established.

  - **May:** Berlin Blockade ends.

  - **October:** Germany is divided into two countries: East and West Germany.

The Cold War (1950–1990)

- **1950–1953:** Korean War; North Korea (supported by China and the USSR) vs. South Korea (supported by the US and UN). This is an economic boost for Japan as a supplier for U.S. forces.

- **1952:** The U.S. occupation of Japan officially ends on April 28th.

- **1953**

    o **March 5:** Death of Joseph Stalin.

    o **July 27:** Korean War armistice signed.

- **1955**

    o **May 14:** The Warsaw Pact is formed as a Soviet counterbalance to NATO. Albania, Bulgaria, Czechoslovakia, East Germany, Hungary, Poland, and Romania are the other signatories.

    o **November 1:** The Vietnam War starts between North Vietnam (supported by the Soviet Union, China, etc.) and South Vietnam, supported by the US and anti-communist allies.

- **1956:** Hungarian Uprising is crushed by Soviet forces.

- **1961:** Construction of the Berlin Wall begins.

- **1962:** The Cuban Missile Crisis brings the world to the brink of nuclear war.

- **1968:** Prague Spring in Czechoslovakia is crushed by Warsaw Pact forces.

- **1973:** Paris Peace Accords are signed, ending U.S. involvement in the Vietnam War.

- **1979:** Soviet invasion of Afghanistan begins.

- **1985:** Mikhail Gorbachev becomes the leader of the Soviet Union, initiating reforms (Perestroika and Glasnost), starting the fall of communist rules in the Soviet Union.

- **1989**

    - **November 9:** The Berlin Wall is pulled down, symbolizing the end of the Cold War.

- **1990**

    - **October 3**: Germany is reunified.

1991: The End of the Cold War

- **December 26:** The Soviet Union officially dissolves, marking the end of the Cold War.

Conclusion

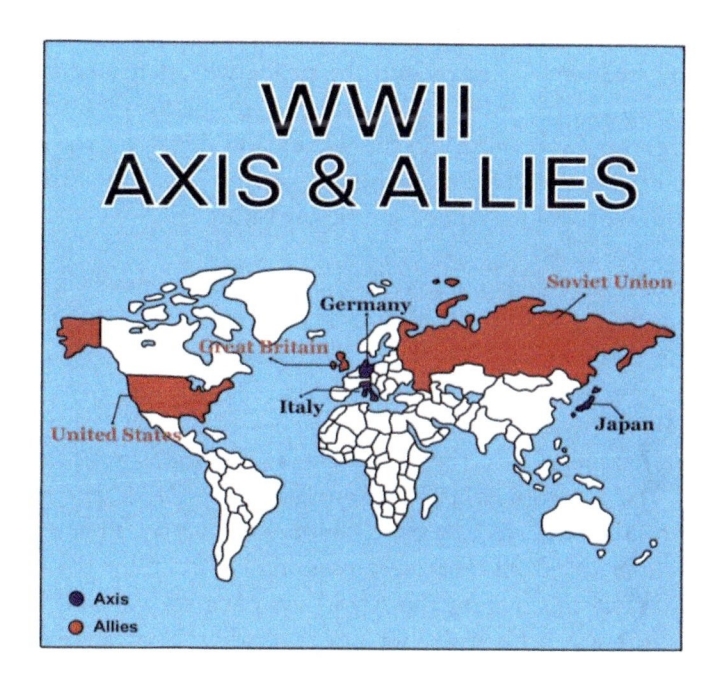

If you're reading this, it means your adventure is complete! Tim and Maya have successfully returned home after an incredible journey through one of the most challenging times in human history—World War II. Now, as they sit back in their own time, they can finally take a deep breath, grateful for what they've learned.

It may be hard to imagine now, but all those events they (and you) witnessed—the battles, the bravery, and the incredible sacrifices—helped shape the world we live in today. From the brave soldiers who fought on the front lines to the everyday people who stood up against injustice, World War II wasn't fought only by famous generals and leaders. It was the courage of millions of ordinary people that made the difference.

Through Tim and Maya, you saw how difficult and frightening those times were. But there was also hope. Even in the darkest moments, people came together to help one another and stand up for what was right. And that's one of the most important lessons of this adventure: When the world feels uncertain, kindness, bravery, and standing up for others can make all the difference.

Sometimes, it's easy to forget how much the past has shaped our lives today. The freedom we enjoy and the peace we often take for granted all come from the lessons and struggles of history. World War II affected nearly every country in the world, and though it was filled with hardship, it also showed us the power of unity and the strength that comes from working together for a better future.

Now that Tim and Maya are back, they'll probably never look at their history books the same way again! They'll remember the real people behind the facts and dates—those who made sacrifices so that future generations could live in peace.

This book has taken you through some of the most important events of World War II, and just like Tim and Maya, you've learned how each moment in history played a part in shaping the world. From the battles in Europe and the Pacific to the rebuilding efforts after the war, every step was crucial in creating the world we have today. And like them, you've come away with a deeper understanding of why remembering the past is so important for the future.

As you close this book, keep Tim and Maya's adventure in mind. History isn't just something that happened long ago—it's something we carry with us every day. And just like the heroes of World War II, we all have the power to make a difference, no matter how small our actions may seem.

Until your next adventure, remember these words by Winston Churchill (n.d.).: "In war, resolution; in defeat, defiance; in victory, magnanimity; in peace, goodwill."

About the Author

Jane Vera is a joyful storyteller, inspiring young minds with enchanting tales. Rooted in a small town, Jane's playful picture books celebrate curiosity and friendship, capturing the magic of childhood. With a focus on learning, Jane encourages imagination, creativity, and dreaming big, helping little ones embrace the wonders of their imagination. Jane Vera is a cherished voice in children's literature, inspiring children to explore and grow both academically and creatively.

Other books for children from the pen of Jane Vera include

- *Revolutionary Quest: A Time-Travel Adventure through America's Past* (April 2024)

- *The Musical Quest: An Adventure Through Sound* (October 2024)

- *The Musical Quest Workbook: An Adventure Through Sound* (October 2024)

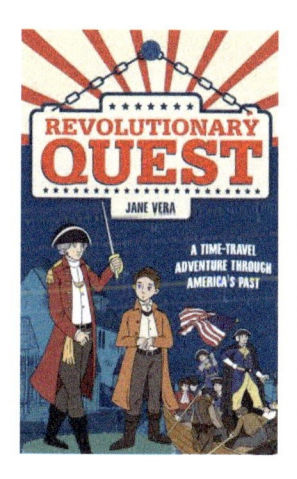

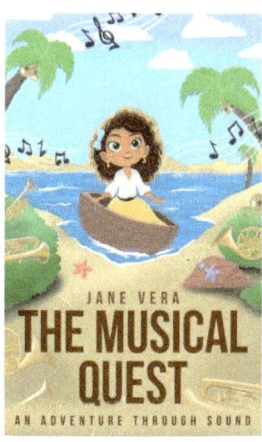

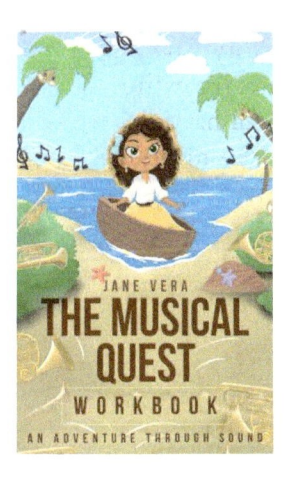

Dear Reader,

I hope Jane Vera's stories have brought a little more joy, wonder, and imagination into your world. I'd love to hear how the book made you feel and what parts sparked your curiosity. Your feedback means the world to me, and it helps others discover the magic of storytelling too.

Leaving a review might seem like a small thing, but it makes a huge difference! It helps more readers find my books and inspires me to keep creating new stories. Plus, I read every single review—yes, each one! Knowing what you loved (or even what you'd like to see more of) helps me grow as an author.

If you have a moment, I'd be so grateful if you could share your thoughts online. Thank you for being part of this journey with me!

With gratitude,
Jane Vera

Quiz Answers

Chapter 1

1. c. Tim and Maya live in New York.

2. c. Tim and Maya were happy because it was a long weekend with Memorial Day falling on Monday.

3. c. Mom wanted them to visit a special exhibition on WWII in the museum.

4. c. The Second World War was fought between 1939–1945.

5. d. Italy was not a part of the Allies. It was an Axis country aligned with Nazi Germany.

Chapter 2

1. a. Tim gave the clock key eight and a half twists to the left because they wanted to travel 85 years into the past.

2. d. They landed in a storage room.

3. b. The streets of London were dark because of a blackout.

4. c. The city was being attacked by Germans in what was called the Blitzkrieg.

5. d. Tim and Maya met Thomas.

Chapter 3

1. a. An Anderson shelter was built outside Thomas's house to protect the family from air raids.

2. d. British citizens were asked to fight by participating in rationing, engaging in factory work, and protecting themselves and their families using government-issued regulations.

3. d. The British government asked the citizens to grow their own vegetables and fruits in "Victory Gardens" in the "Dig for Victory" campaign to both reduce the shortage of food caused by the lack of imports during the time and give the people a purposeful hobby that would keep them happy during the war.

4. c. The Blackouts in the cities reduced the visibility of the German bombers.

5. c. France became occupied territory under the Germans in June 1940.

Chapter 4

1. c. PM Churchill's speech was being broadcast on the wireless.

2. c. Churchill was called the English Bulldog because he was ferocious and focused on fighting the enemies during the war.

3. c. The Battle of Britain was fought in the skies above Britain.

4. a. Today, Churchill is remembered most for his brilliant oratory in keeping up the British morale.

5. b. England was never invaded by Germany.

Chapter 5

1. a. The Germans sent their messages and plans from one place to another through coded messages using radio signals.

2. c. The huts at Bletchley Park were where coded information was divided based on where it came from.

3. c. Alan Turing headed Hut 8.

4. b. The Ultra helped the British understand crucial German military movements and plans.

5. d. *Cryptanalyst* is another term for a codebreaker.

Chapter 6

1. d. Munition factories were where weapons and arms were made.

2. c. Woolwich was on the bank of River Thames.

3. d. The ordnance factory Tim and Maya visited was located in an old house called Tower Place.

4. d. Princess Elizabeth, who later became Queen Elizabeth II, was an early recruit of the ATS.

5. d. Active combat was never given to British women during WWII.

Chapter 7

1. b. On December 8, 1941, America declared war on Japan.

2. b. Japan planned the attack on Pearl Harbor in advance because the Japanese fleet moved out of their harbor in November 1941 to attack Pearl Harbor on December 7th.

3. b. Admiral Isoroku Yamamoto was the architect of the Pearl Harbor attack.

4. d. The American population and government did not want a war until the Pearl Harbor attack because their economy was weak, they did not want to get involved in a European War, and they thought it best to build up defenses first.

5. a. Pearl Harbor is located on the island of Oahu.

Chapter 8

1. c. *Hiryu* was the last Japanese carrier to sink.

2. c. Over 3,000 Japanese men were lost in the Battle of Midway.

3. b. The Dauntless bombers helped the Americans.

4. a. The Japanese launched a diversionary attack on the Aleutian Islands.

5. b. The Battle of Midway lasted for three days.

Chapter 9

1. c. The German General Erwin Rommel was called the "Desert Fox."

2. d. America provided the Sherman Tanks and other weaponry during the Battle of El Alamein.

3. b. Operation Lightfoot and Operation Supercharge were part of the Battle of El Alamein.

4. c. The Operation that made use of heavy artillery firing and attacking infantrymen to break into the German line was Operation Supercharge.

5. a. Winston Churchill called El Alamein the "end of the beginning" because he was sure the beginning of WWII was ending and the tide was turning in the favor of the Allies.

Chapter 10

1. c. The Free French Army Commander was Charles de Gaulle.

2. d. The Allies did not use the tactic of printing wrong information in newspapers to confuse the Germans.

3. c. D-Day meant the day (of attack).

4. b. Dwight Eisenhower was the American General who fought as the Supreme Commander of the Allied Forces. He went on to become the president of America later.

5. d. Paris is also called the City of Lights.

Chapter 11

1. b. The holocaust was the mass imprisonment, torture, or killing of Jews and others under Nazi Germany.

2. c. Berlin was not a German prisoner camp.

3. c. Heinrich Himmler was the "Architect of the Holocaust."

4. d. The first prisoner camp to be liberated was Majdanek.

5. d. The Jews were identified and first taken to ghettoes, which were districts where they were held.

Chapter 12

1. c. Victory Day in Western Europe was on May 8, 1945.

2. c. Hitler used the air raid shelter beneath his chancellery in Berlin.

3. c. Italy did not control a zone in post-WWII Germany.

4. b. Hitler married Eva Braun.

5. d. Alfred Jodl was the first German General to sign the document of German surrender with the Allies.

Chapter 13

1. c. Robert J. Oppenheimer is the Father of the Atomic Bomb.

2. c. Hiroshima and Nagasaki were the two cities on which the atomic bombs were dropped.

3. d. President Harry Truman of the US agreed to the dropping of the atomic bomb.

4. b. Brigadier General Leslie R. Groves Jr. was the director of the Manhattan Project.

5. d. The dropping of the two atomic bombs ensured Japan's surrender, ending the war.

Chapter 14

1. a. Germany was always divided into four zones by the Allies until its reunification in 1990. This statement is untrue because Germany became two countries by 1949.

2. c. Joseph Stalin was the Premier of Soviet Russia.

3. d. Finland was not a NATO member when it was established in 1949.

4. c. The "Iron Curtain" was the difference in ideas between the East and West Blocs, causing political tension during the Cold War.

5. d. East Germany followed the communist policies of the USSR.

References

Battle of Midway. (2022). The National WWII Museum. https://www.nationalww2museum.org/war/topics/battle-of-midway#:~:text=had

BBC. (2014). *World Wars: Second Battle of El Alamein.* BBC. https://www.bbc.co.uk/history/worldwars/wwtwo/ff5_second_alamein.shtml

Berlin after 1945. (n.d.). Berlin-the Official Website of Berlin. https://www.berlin.de/en/history/8481782-8619314-berlin-after-1945.en.html#:~:text=Large%20parts%20of%20the%20city

Berlin after World War II Geographic. (n.d.). PBS. https://www.pbs.org/wgbh/americanexperience/features/nuremberg-berlin-gallery/

Bletchley Park facts for kids. (2017). Kiddle. https://kids.kiddle.co/Bletchley_Park

Churchill, W. (1940, September 11). Every man to his post. *National Churchill Museum* [Wireless Broadcast to London]. https://www.nationalchurchillmuseum.org/every-man-to-his-post.html

Churchill, W. (n.d.). *A quote from The Second World War.* Goodreads.com. https://www.goodreads.com/quotes/261261-in-war-resolution-in-defeat-defiance-in-victory-magnanimity-in

D-Day on land: The Allied landings in Normandy. (n.d.). Imperial War Museums. https://www.iwm.org.uk/history/d-day-on-land-the-allied-landings-in-normandy

Dippold, T. (2023, August 29). *10 little known facts about the Holocaust.* Holocaust Memorial Resource & Education - Center of

Florida. https://www.holocaustedu.org/blog/little-known-facts-about-the-holocaust/

Editors of Encyclopaedia (2024, September 7). *Manhattan Project*. Encyclopedia Britannica. https://www.britannica.com/event/Manhattan-Project

Editors of Encyclopaedia (2024, September 10). *Cold War*. Encyclopedia Britannica. https://www.britannica.com/event/Cold-War

FDR's "Day of Infamy" speech: Crafting a call to arms. (2001). *Prologue Magazine*, *33*(4). National Archives. https://www.archives.gov/publications/prologue/2001/winter/crafting-day-of-infamy-speech.html

Frost, N. (2020, June 5). *As the Allies closed in on Hitler, they jockeyed for future world dominance*. HISTORY. https://www.history.com/news/end-wwii-race-to-berlin-1945-atomic-scientists

Gilbert, A. (2018). *Battles of El-Alamein*. Encyclopedia Britannica. https://www.britannica.com/event/battles-of-El-Alamein

Haglund, D. G. (2024, September 10). *North Atlantic Treaty Organization*. Encyclopedia Britannica. https://www.britannica.com/topic/North-Atlantic-Treaty-Organization

H-Hour: D-Day historical overview. (2019). The United States Army. https://www.army.mil/d-day/history.html

History.com Editors. (2018, August 21). *Paris liberated*. HISTORY. https://www.history.com/this-day-in-history/paris-liberated

History.com Editors. (2019, October 21). *Battle of Midway*. History; A&E Television Networks. https://www.history.com/topics/world-war-ii/battle-of-midway

Impressive facts about the historic Battle Of Midway. (2019). PastFactory. https://www.pastfactory.com/history/battle-of-midway/#:~:text=Both%20sides

Keegan, J. (2024, July 29). *Normandy invasion.* Encyclopedia Britannica. https://www.britannica.com/event/Normandy-Invasion

Kelly, J. (2014, March 31). The six key moments of the Cold War relived. *BBC News.* https://www.bbc.com/news/magazine-26788606

Little Boy and Fat Man. (2014, July 23). Atomic Heritage Foundation. https://ahf.nuclearmuseum.org/ahf/history/little-boy-and-fat-man/

Major Cold War events. (n.d.). Student Center Encyclopedia Britannica. https://www.britannica.com/study/major-cold-war-events

Manhattan Project - Manhattan Project National Historical Park. (2024). U.S. National Park Service. https://www.nps.gov/mapr/learn/manhattan-project.htm#:~:text=The%20Manhattan

National Geographic. (2016, August 8). *Attack on Pearl Harbor.* National Geographic Kids. https://kids.nationalgeographic.com/history/article/pearl-harbor

The 1940s house. (2017). Imperial War Museums. https://www.iwm.org.uk/learning/resources/the-1940s-house

Nix, E. (2018, September). *Were they always called World War I and World War II?* HISTORY. https://www.history.com/news/were-they-always-called-world-war-i-and-world-war-ii

The aftermath - Pearl Harbor after the attack. (2016, October 23). PearlHarbor. https://pearlharbor.org/blog/aftermath-pearl-harbor-attack/

Ramos, J. (2014). *Barrage Balloons.* World War Two. https://www.worldwar-two.net/weapons/barrage_balloons/#:~:text=The%20barrage

Ray, M. (2024, May 27). *Battle of Midway.* Encyclopedia Britannica. https://www.britannica.com/event/Battle-of-Midway

Sir Winston Churchill's Speeches. (2019). America's National Churchill Museum. https://www.nationalchurchillmuseum.org/winston-churchills-speeches.html

Swift, J. (2024, June 18). *Battle of Berlin.* Encyclopedia Britannica. https://www.britannica.com/topic/Battle-of-Berlin

Printed in Great Britain
by Amazon